How to Form a Limited Company for £50

How to Form a Limited Company for £50
—Without the Aid of a Solicitor

BARRY M. SHEPPARD

COMPLETE WITH SPECIMEN FORMS,
MEMORANDUM AND ARTICLES OF ASSOCIATION

London
GEORGE ALLEN & UNWIN
Sydney Boston

First published by George Allen & Unwin 1986

George Allen & Unwin (Publishers) Ltd
40 Museum Street, London WC1A 1LU, UK

George Allen & Unwin (Publishers) Ltd
Park Lane, Hemel Hempstead, Herts HP2 4TE, UK

George Allen & Unwin Australia Pty Ltd
8 Napier Street, North Sydney, NSW 2060, Australia

George Allen & Unwin with the
Port Nicholson Press
PO Box 11-838 Wellington, New Zealand

Allen & Unwin Inc.,
8 Winchester Place, Winchester, Mass. 01890, USA

This publication is designed to provide accurate and authoritative information. It is sold with the understanding that the publisher is not engaged in rendering legal, accounting or other professional service. If legal advice or other expert assistance is required, the services of a competent professional person should be sought. Prices and fees quoted in this book may be increased without notice by the government and other bodies and should be used only as a guide.

British Library Cataloguing in Publication Data

Sheppard, Barry
How to form a limited company for £50.
1. New business enterprises – Great Britain
2. Limited liability – Great Britain
I. Title
338.7'4'0941 HD62.5
ISBN 0–04–338136–7

Library of Congress Cataloging-in-Publication Data

Sheppard, Barry M.
How to form a limited company for £50.
1. Corporation law – Great Britain. 2. Incorporation – Great Britain.
I. Title.
KD2079.S5 1986 346.41'066 85–28614
ISBN 0–04–338136–7 344.10666

Set in 11 on 12 point Palatino by Bedford Typesetters Ltd
and printed in Great Britain by Mackays of Chatham Ltd

Acknowledgements

I'd like to thank the capable staff at Companies House in Cardiff, especially Mrs J. A. Ceasar, Mrs K. Street and Miss J. M. Henry who have been more than helpful; Ann for typing various drafts in a very professional manner; Nick Brealey, my editor, and Liz Paton for their help; Shelley, my wife, for her assistance.

It is not the critic who counts or the man who points out how the strong man stumbled or where the doer of deeds could have done better. The credit belongs to the man who is actually in the arena, whose face is marred by dust, sweat and blood – who strives valiantly – who errs and comes short again – who knows the great enthusiasms, the great devotions and who spends himself in a worthy cause – who at the best knows the triumph of high achievement and who at the worst at least fails while doing greatly. His place shall never be with those cold, timid souls who know neither victory nor defeat.

HERE'S TO ENTREPRENEURS

Contents

1

Private Registered Companies

There are three basic ways to operate a business:

- *The sole proprietorship* (the 'bachelor' or 'maiden')
  The individual has full responsibility for running the business and takes the profit. S/he is liable for all debts and obligations to the extent of his or her own personal wealth.

- *The partnership* (the 'marriage')
  Two or more proprietors share the profits and *each* is equally responsible for *all* its debts, not merely his or her investments in it. Most partnerships fall apart because at the inception there wasn't a properly drawn-up partnership agreement. Liken a partnership to a marriage – it is a serious matter and requires a lot of thought.

- *The limited company*
  A limited company is a separate legal entity created by two or more people. It is able to enter into contracts, own property and incur liabilities. Its shareholders have no liability beyond what they may owe on the

shares (unless they give a personal guarantee). A limited company has a never-ending life unless it is closed down by the shareholders or is forced to close down by bankruptcy.

I believe in positive thinking. Having said that, businesses do fail, and if you fail as an individual it's difficult to start again. I have seen so many families torn apart by bankruptcy and the loss of everything they possess that I feel all new and existing entrepreneurs should have the protection of a limited liability company. The limited company, if run legally and lawfully, is a powerful protection of your family assets. Solicitors' fees for the formation of a company range from £200 to £1500 or more. However, an individual can legally incorporate his own company without the aid of a solicitor. It is a relatively simple task, speedy (three to four weeks from application) and cheap. This book enables the reader to incorporate at the lowest possible cost by giving all specimen forms, necessary documentation and information for the running of the corporation.

I have used the word 'incorporate' in the previous paragraph, so let us look in the dictionary for the meaning that we shall be using for it:

Incorporate – to form into one body: to unite: to blend: to associate with another whole: to form into a legal body or corporation.
Incorporated – united in one body.
Incorporation – a body of individuals authorized to act as a single person.

What are the advantages of forming a limited company?

- *Personal liability*
  The directors'/shareholders' liability is limited to the

amount of the issued share capital. If a director/shareholder has paid for his issued shares he cannot be held personally liable for the debts of the company. The directors'/shareholders' personal assets cannot be touched. When a limited company is put into liquidation, through not meeting its liabilities, the directors/shareholders are free to commence business again either in their own right or through another company (providing a criminal act hasn't been committed).

- *Protection of name*
  Once your company name is registered, it is protected by law. No one else is allowed to use it. (See also Chapter 3, sections 3.6 and 3.7.)

- *Separate legal entity*
  The company is quite distinct from its members. The death or personal bankruptcy of a director will not affect the company's continuity.

- *Employees*
  Incentives can be given to them by means of profit-sharing through minority shares. They can become directors as an added status but can be removed any time.

- *Security for money borrowed*
  A wide range of securities can be offered as collateral. It can issue debentures for security.

- The management structure is clearly defined.

- The disposal of the whole or part of the business is easily arranged.

- There can be tax advantages.

The opportunities offered to the trader are thus many and obvious. A critic may object that they tempt the individual to escape his legitimate personal liabilities. Whether this be so or not, however, it is sufficient that the law stands as it does; notwithstanding any occasional opportunities it may offer for immoral commercial enterprise, the system of limited liability affords, on the whole, undoubted and most necessary advantages and facilities to trade and commerce generally.

As at 15 December 1984 there were approximately 999,900 live companies on the registers of England and Wales, and Scotland. The number of new companies incorporated every year within Great Britain has been on the increase, with 1984 being a record:

1979 – 62,958
1980 – 66,104
1981 – 68,941
1982 – 82,955
1983 – 91,470
1984 – 97,908

During 1985, approximately 2000 companies per week were being incorporated.

At this stage it is useful to understand a little of the history of incorporation, at the same time giving you an introduction to the private company before we proceed.

Before 1844, incorporation was either by Royal Charter granted by the Crown or by Special Act of Parliament. The Joint Stock Companies Act 1844 enabled companies to gain statutory recognition by a simple act of registration by the newly established Companies Registration Offices, set up separately in England and Wales and in Scotland. The concept of limited liability was introduced by the Limited Liability Act 1855, and subsequently companies were obliged to re-register under the Joint Stock Companies Act 1856. (Since that consolidating Act, nearly 2 million companies have been incorporated.) There were various amendments to the Limited Liability Act 1855 until the Companies Act 1948. There were five Companies Acts (1948, 1967, 1976, 1980 and 1981) in force until the Companies Act 1985, which contains 747 sections and 25 schedules and repeals, and consolidates in one volume the whole of company legislation formerly contained in the five previous acts and in the Companies (Floating Charge) (Scotland) Act 1972 and in the Companies (Beneficial Interests) Act 1983.

It is the private company with which we are going to deal. The public company (which we discuss in only minor detail) is a major undertaking and should be created only with the help of expert advice. A private company is a company that is not a public company – it cannot offer shares or debentures to the public (cash or otherwise). The company may be limited by shares (the most common form), limited by guarantee (usually a professional body or non-trading company) or unlimited (very rare).

All companies are formed and approved by Companies Registration Offices. The current functions of the Companies Registration Offices are threefold: to incorporate and dissolve companies; to examine and file documents required by the Companies Acts to be delivered to the Registrar; and to make this information available for public inspection. The first function is the subject of the following chapters; the other functions are dealt with in Appendix B.

Before I guide you through the various procedures and regulations involved in an application for registration I have set out the main points for the formation of your new company. It is intended to show you that it is SIMPLICITY itself.

The procedure for forming a new limited company (simplified)

- Make a written application for the necessary free forms (see specimen letter, p. 42).
- Establish acceptability of selected name.
- Draft Memorandum and Articles of Association, tailor-made to your own business (see specimens, pp. 49–62).
- Fill in forms: No PUC1, No 10 and No 12 (see specimens, pp. 43–48).
- Send off to the Companies Registration Office:

  (a) Completed forms No PUC1, No 10, No 12.
  (b) Registration fee of £50.
  (c) Draft copy of Memorandum and Articles of Association.

- When approved you receive your Certificate of Incorporation.

SIMPLE?

Let me assure you it is.

Chapter 2 deals with the selection and approval of company names. Chapter 3 covers rules and regulations concerning incorporation, the forms involved and a draft Memorandum and Articles of Association. Following this we have the arrival of the certificate of incorporation and the matters relating to it (Chapter 4). For tax purposes and companies wanting anonymity I have included a chapter on company formation in offshore areas (Chapter 5). Finally, Chapter 6 gives you an insight into the procedures that need to be adopted if you have a company registered overseas and wish to establish a place of business in Great Britain.

2

Company Names

2.1 Get a Good Name

A GOOD NAME IS IMPORTANT. You're identifying yourself to your potential customers and presenting the image your business holds. Ideally, your name should relate to the business itself and be 'catchy'. Which business name would you remember:

OINCK OINCK Ltd or DAVIS PIGS Ltd?

What about these – see how they relate to a particular business?

City Bag Stores (bags)
You're putting me on (clothes)
Jack Rabbit Press (for fast reproductions)
Message Minders (answering service)
Ticket Master (travel agent)

These sorts of names conjure up your type of business in the mind of the receiver of your business card, etc., and are unlikely to be forgotten. So, choose carefully and remember

YOU NEVER GET A SECOND CHANCE TO MAKE A FIRST IMPRESSION

Important

There is a distinction between being able to trade under a name and being able to incorporate a company under it. Many names are already registered as trade marks. A trade mark is the name or symbol by which goods of a particular company can be identified by the public and is usually registered with the Registrar of Trade Marks. Care must be taken not to choose a company name that infringes anyone's trademark (see Chapter 3, sections 3.6 and 3.7).

2.2 How to Register a Company Name

The Companies Act 1981 simplified the requirements relating to company names, but it is now particularly important that persons forming companies should satisfy themselves in advance of the acceptability of the proposed name, bearing in mind that an objection might be received that could result in the company being directed to change its name (see section 2.4). It will no longer be possible for the Registrar to give provisional name approval except in cases where the prior approval of the Secretary of State for Trade is specifically required.

Broadly, a company name will not be registered if:

- it is the same as or too like (see section 2.3) a name

already appearing on the Index of Company Names maintained by the Registrar of Companies;

- it contains the words 'Limited', 'Unlimited' or 'Public Limited Company', or their Welsh equivalents, or abbreviations of these words, except at the end of the name;
- in the opinion of the Secretary of State it is offensive;
- in the opinion of the Secretary of State its use would constitute a criminal offence.

In addition, the approval of the Secretary of State is required before a company may be registered by a name that includes certain words or expressions (see section 2.5).

Applicants are advised to check whether the name proposed is the same as one already registered by referring to the Index, which can be inspected free of charge in the Public Search Rooms at Cardiff, Edinburgh and London and at many main libraries. In determining whether one name is the same as another, certain words and their abbreviations, together with accents and punctuation marks, will be disregarded. These words include the definite article and the words 'Company', 'Limited', 'Public Limited Company', etc., and their Welsh equivalents, whilst 'and' and '&' will be taken to be the same. Names that are phonetically identical but not visually identical will be allowed as not being 'the same as'.

If the name is not the same as one already on the Index, and does not require the prior approval of the Secretary of State (see section 2.5), the incorporation documents (or, in the case of a change of name, the necessary special resolution) should be submitted to the appropriate Registrar of Companies (see Chapter 3). If the name is acceptable within the provisions of the Act and the documents are correctly completed, the company name will then be registered and the Certificate of Incorporation issued.

2.3 'Too Like' Names

In considering whether names are 'too like', the Secretary of State must be prepared to take account of all factors that may be considered to suggest similarity and lead to confusion between the names of two companies. These will include, for example, the nature and location of the businesses concerned.

Subject to this requirement, names may be considered to be 'too like':

- if the names are phonetically identical;
- if there is only an insignificant variation in the spelling of the two names;
- if, in the case of an overseas company registered under Part XXIII of the Companies Act 1985, the names differ from a name already on the index only by the substitution of the overseas country equivalent of 'Limited', 'Unlimited', 'Public Limited Company';
- if the names contain a word or words that might be regarded as distinctive elements, unless that element is qualified in such a way as would minimise risk of confusion. A distinctive element will normally be defined as 'made-up words', 'non-dictionary words', 'combinations of two or more letters used as a prefix'. In some cases, everyday words used in a 'distinctive' way may also be considered as distinctive elements. Place names or everyday descriptive words in general use will not normally be regarded as distinctive.

Similar descriptive elements – e.g. press/printing, staff agency/employment agency – for the inclusion in one name of only a general or 'weak' qualification such as 'holding', 'group', 'system', 'services', etc., would not normally be regarded as a sufficient qualification.

Examples

Names that are the same:

MAYFAIR ENGINEERING LIMITED v MAYFAIR ENGINEERING COMPANY, LIMITED

Names that are phonetically identical:

LYFESTYLE LIMITED v LIFESTYLE LIMITED

AB-CHEM LIMITED v ABKEM LIMITED

Names in which the slight variation in spelling does not make a significant difference:

CONSOLAIR LTD v CONSULAIR LTD

Names that contain the same distinctive element:

(a) where the names are sufficiently qualified:

FACTROMATIC COMPUTERS LIMITED v FACTROMATIC PLANT HIRE LIMITED

(b) where the names are not sufficiently qualified:

MACHALA LIMITED v MECHALA HOLDING LIMITED

ODDBODS PRESS LIMITED v ODDBODS PRINTING LIMITED

Names that are 'like' where other factors may be relevant:

PLAN TRAVEL LIMITED v PLANNED TRAVEL LIMITED

2.4 Directions to Change a Company's Name

The Secretary of State has certain powers to direct a company to change its name. A company can be directed to change its name within twelve months of its registration if it is 'the same as' or, in the opinion of the Secretary of State, 'too like' a name appearing in the Index of Company Names at the time of registration. Such names will normally be brought to the Secretary of State's attention by objections being lodged by any person who may feel that the name is 'the same as' or 'too like' that of a previously registered company. Objections should be submitted to the Registrar, giving reasons in full and including any available evidence of confusion that has arisen. Details of the criteria that the Secretary of State will apply for directions on 'too like' names are given in section 2.3 above. It is important therefore that, before applying for registration of a name, applicants consider carefully whether its acceptance could lead to a complaint from another company, and the possibility that it may be subject to a change of name direction after incorporation. This aspect will not form a part of the Department of Trade's consideration when examining the name before registration.

A company can also be directed to change its name within five years of the date of registration where it appears to the Secretary of State that the company has provided misleading information for the purposes of registration, or has given undertakings or assurances for that purpose that have not been fulfilled.

Finally, Section 32 of the Companies Act 1985 provides powers for a company to be directed to change its name if the name gives so misleading an indication of the nature of the company's activities as to be likely to cause harm to the public.

2.5 Secretary of State Approval

For all names that require the approval of the Secretary of State, applicants should seek the advice of the Companies Registration Office either in Cardiff (for companies intending to have their registered office in England or Wales), or in Edinburgh (for companies intending to have their registered office in Scotland). Details about the requirements on the use of the name will then be sent to the applicant.

The following words and expressions will require the consent of the Secretary of State for Trade before their use will be allowed in a company name. If the name includes any of these words or expressions, further information will probably be required to support the application and the applicant will be advised accordingly.

Words that imply national or international pre-eminence:

British
England
English
European
Great Britain
International
Ireland
Irish
National
Scotland
Scottish
United Kingdom
Wales
Welsh

Words that imply governmental patronage or sponsorship:

Authority
Board
Council

Words that imply business pre-eminence or representative status:

Association
Federation
Institute
Institution
Society

Words that imply specific objects or functions:

Assurance/Assurer
Benevolent
Building Society
Chamber of Commerce/Industry/Trade
Charter/Chartered
Co-operative
Foundation
Friendly
Fund
Giro
Group
Holdings
Insurance/Insurer
Patent/Patentee
Register/Registered
Reinsurer
Stock Exchange
Trust

If the name contains any of the following words or expressions, applicants will be required to ask the relevant body, in writing, whether (and if so why) it has any objections to the proposal to use the word or expression in the name. A statement that such a request has been made, together with the appropriate registration documents, should then be submitted to the Companies Registration Office. Normally a company would be registered by a name containing any of these words or expressions only if the applicant has obtained a letter of non-objection from the relevant department or body. Any correspondence should be submitted with the appropriate registration documents.

Word or expression	Relevant body for companies intending to have registered office in England or Wales	Relevant body for companies intending to have registered office in Scotland
Royal, Royale, Royalty, King, Queen, Prince, Princess, Duke, Windsor, His/Her Majesty	E2 Division (Room 820), Home Office, Queen Anne's Gate, London SW1H 9AT	Scottish Home & Health Department, Old St Andrews House, Edinburgh EH1 3DE
Police	F1 Division, Police Department, Home Office, Queen Anne's Gate, London SW1H 9AT	Police Division, Scottish Home & Health Department, Old St Andrews House, Edinburgh EH1 3DE
Special School	Schools II Branch, Department of Education and Science, Elizabeth House, York Road, London SE1 7PH	As for England & Wales
Contact Lens	The Registrar, General Optical Council, 41 Harley Street, London W1N 2DJ	As for England & Wales
Dental, Dentistry	The Registrar, General Dental Council, 37 Wimpole Street, London W1M 8DQ	As for England & Wales
Nurse, Nursing	The Secretary, General Nursing Council for England & Wales, 23 Portland Place, London W1A 1BA	The Registrar, General Nursing Council for Scotland, 5 Dranaway Street, Edinburgh EH3 6DP
Midwife, Midwifery	The Secretary, Central Midwives Board, 39 Harrington Gardens, London SW7	The Secretary, Central Midwives Board for Scotland, 24 Dublin Street, Edinburgh EH1 3PU

Word or expression	Relevant body for companies intending to have registered office in England or Wales	Relevant body for companies intending to have registered office in Scotland
Health Visitor	The Secretary, Council for Education and Training of Health Visitors, Clifton House, Euston Road, London NW1 2RS	As for England & Wales
District Nurse	M. L. Godfrey, Panel of Assessors in District Nurse Training, Room 706, Hannibal House, Elephant & Castle, London SE1 6TE	As for England & Wales
Health Centre	Mrs F. V. Rogers, Division PPIA, Room C205, Department of Health & Social Security, Alexander Fleming House, Elephant & Castle, London SE1 6BY	As for England & Wales
Health Service	Mr A. G. Saville, HS2D Division, Department of Health & Social Security, Alexander Fleming House, Elephant & Castle, London SE1 6BY	As for England & Wales
Nursing Home	HS3A Division, Department of Health & Social Security, Room 1221, Hannibal House, Elephant & Castle, London SE1 6TE	As for England & Wales

Word or expression	Relevant body for companies intending to have registered office in England or Wales	Relevant body for companies intending to have registered office in Scotland
Pregnancy Termination, Abortion	HS1C Division, Department of Health & Social Security, Room C214, Alexander Fleming House, Elephant & Castle, London SE1 6BY	As for England & Wales
Breed, Breeder	Animal Health II Division, Ministry of Agriculture, Fisheries & Foods, Tolworth Tower, Surbiton, Surrey KT6 7DX	As for England & Wales
Charity, Charitable	Registration Division, Charity Commission, 14 Ryder Street, St James's, London SW1Y 6AH	Civil Law & Charities, Scottish Home & Health Department, St Andrews House, Edinburgh
Apothecary	The Worshipful Society of Apothecaries of London, Apothecaries Hall, Blackfriars Lane, London EC4	The Pharmaceutical Society of Great Britain, 1 Lambeth High Street, London SE1 7JN
University, Polytechnic	FHE3, Department of Education & Science, Elizabeth House, York Road, London SE1 7PH	As for England & Wales

The use of certain words in company names is covered by other legislation and their improper use may constitute a criminal offence (see Section 26(d) of the Companies Act 1985). Those known to the Department of Trade are listed below, together with details of the relevant legislation. Applicants wishing to use any of these words may be asked to seek confirmation from the relevant body listed that the use of the word does not contravene the relevant legislation. The Department of Trade also reserves the right to seek advice in each case direct with the relevant body if necessary.

Word or expression	Relevant legislation	Relevant body
Architect, Architectural	Section 1, Architects Registration Act 1938	The Registrar, Architects Registration Council of the United Kingdom, 73 Hallam Street, London W1N 6EE
Credit Union	Credit Union Act 1979	The Registrar of Friendly Societies, 17 North Audley Street, London W1Y 2AP
Veterinary Surgeon	Sections 19/20, Veterinary Surgeons Act 1966	The Registrar, Royal College of Veterinary Surgeons, 32 Belgrave Square, London SW1X 8QP
Dentist, Dental Surgeon, Dental Practitioner	Sections 38/39, Dentist Act 1957	The Registrar, General Dental Council, 37 Wimpole Street, London W1M 8DQ
Drug, Druggist, Pharmaceutical, Pharmaceutist, Pharmacist, Pharmacy	Section 78, Medicines Act 1968	Pharmaceutical Society of Great Britain, 1 Lambeth High Street, London SE1 7JN
Ophthalmic/ Dispensing/ Registered Optician	Sections 4 & 22, Opticians Act 1958	The Registrar, General Optical Council, 41 Harley Street, London W1N 2DJ

Word or expression	Relevant legislation	Relevant body
Bank, Banker, Banking Deposit	Banking Act 1979	Bank of England, Threadneedle Street, London EC2R 8AM
Red Cross	Geneva Convention Act 1957	Seek advice of CRO
Anzac	Section, Anzac Act 1916	Seek advice of CRO
Insurance Broker, Assurance Broker, Re-Insurance Broker, Re-Assurance Broker	Sections 2 & 3, Insurance Brokers (Registration) Act	Seek advice of CRO

Finally, the Secretary of State's approval is required of a name that gives the impression that the company is connected with HM Government or any local authority. Such names will be allowed only where a genuine connection with HM Government or local authority can be shown. The use of such words as 'parliament', 'department', 'centre', 'government' could in certain circumstances imply such a connection.

2.6 Companies Wishing to Be Exempt from the Requirement to Use the Word 'Limited' in the Company Name

For many years, companies legislation has permitted charitable and certain other types of companies to omit the word 'Limited' from their name even though they had limited liability, but this was subject to the granting of a specific licence under Section 19 of the Companies Act 1948. Since 22 December 1980, no public company has been able to take advantage of this licensing system and the Companies Act 1981 abolished it completely as from 26 February 1982. From that date, however, any existing or proposed private company that is limited by guarantee, and that can satisfy the requirements of Section 25 of the Act as described below, will be permitted to omit the word 'Limited' from its name, either by change of name or on incorporation as a new company. Private companies (whether limited by guarantee or shares) that already have a licence can continue to enjoy this privilege so long as they conform to the requirements described below. Any company that has a licence under Section 19 but does not meet the requirements of Section 25 of the new Act was required to change its name by resolution of its directors within twelve months from 26 February 1982 or change its constitution so as to comply with the new requirements. (Now covered by Section 30 of the Companies Act 1985.)

What requirements must be satisfied

The requirements are described in Section 30 of the Companies Act 1985. The objects of the company must be the promotion of commerce, art, science, education, religion, charity or any profession and anything incidental or conducive to any of these objects. The Memorandum or Articles of Association of the company must:

- require its profits or other income to be applied in promoting its objects;
- prohibit the payment of dividends to its members; and

- require the net assets of the company, if it is wound up, to be transferred to another body either with objects similar to its own, or whose objects are the promoting of a charity.

What action the company must take

A statutory declaration in the prescribed form may be completed to the effect that the company satisfies the appropriate requirements. The Registrar may refuse to register a company by a name that omits the word 'Limited' unless a declaration is sent. Copies of Form 30(5)(a), for a new corporation, and Form 30(5)(c), on change of name, can be obtained free of charge from Companies Registration Offices in Cardiff and Edinburgh. When completed, the form should be submitted to the appropriate Companies Registration Office, together with the incorporation documents if the Company is being newly formed. If the company is already registered, the form should be accompanied by a special resolution changing the name of the company to omit the word 'Limited'.

What additional benefits are available

Companies to which the new provisions apply are also exempt from the requirements of Sections 345–50 of the Companies Act 1985 relating to the publishing of their names and the sending of lists of members to the Registrar of Companies.

What restrictions apply to this category of company

Companies must not subsequently alter their Memorandum or Articles so that they no longer meet the requirements to omit 'Limited' from their name. The making of any such alteration is a criminal offence, and the Act prescribes penalties for any such contravention. The Secretary of State has powers to direct a company to change its name by resolution of the directors and reinsert the word 'Limited' if it appears to him that it has carried on any business other than the promotion of any of the objects stated above, or has applied any of its profits or other income other than in promoting such objects, or has paid a dividend to any of its members. The Act also provides penalties for failure to comply with any such direction.

Is a fee payable?
For new incorporation, the normal incorporation fee of £50 only is required. For a change of name, no fee is payable if the change is confined solely to removal of the word 'Limited' from the name; in all other cases, a fee of £40 is required.

General information
These provisions do not exempt a company from complying with Section 9(7) of the European Communities Act 1972, under the terms of which a company is required to mention on all business letters and order forms the fact that it is a limited company.

2.7 Overseas Companies

The names of overseas companies registered under Section 691 of the Companies Act 1985 are subject to the same provisions as apply to British registered companies. If the name is not acceptable, the company will receive a Notice to change its name.

2.8 Summary

For the purpose of this exercise let us create two imaginary people who wish to go into business together. They are: Mr Jack Daniels and Mrs Hilary Evans, and they have decided to form a limited company.

(1) They decide on a name:

THE BUSINESS BOOK CLUB LIMITED

(2) They check at their local library or Companies House:

• does the name already appear?	Yes/No
• is it too like another name:	Yes/No
• does it require approval?	Yes/No
• is it offensive?	Yes/No
• could it constitute a criminal offence?	Yes/No

(3) Everything checks out – the company will be called THE BUSINESS BOOK CLUB LIMITED

They are now ready to submit the incorporation documents. You will find specimens of these on pp. 43–62.

3

Incorporation of New Companies

Let us first look at the regulations concerning the incorporation of new companies. Under companies legislation, any two or more persons, associated for a lawful purpose, may form an incorporated company with or without limited liability. There are four types of company:

- *a private company limited by shares* – where the liability is limited to the amount of share capital its members have agreed to pay;
- *a private company limited by guarantee* – where the liability is limited to the amount its members have undertaken to contribute to the assets of the company, in the event of it being wound up. No company formed as, or becoming, a company limited by guarantee may have a share capital.
- *a private unlimited company* – where there is no limit to the liability of its members;
- *a public company*, which must be incorporated with a share capital of at least the authorized minimum,

£50,000. At least a quarter of this must be paid up when the company is formed.

Remember that a very high proportion of private businesses trade in the form of the limited company.

3.1 Public Companies

A public company may be formed only as a company limited by shares. The provisions of the Companies Act in relation to its registration as a public company must have been complied with.

The following documents must be delivered to the Registrar of Companies in connection with the registration of a new public company.

(1) Memorandum of Association

(i) The Memorandum of a public company limited by shares must contain the following details:

- (a) the name of the company;
- (b) a statement that the company is to be a public company;
- (c) a statement of the situation of the registered office of the company, i.e. whether it is to be in England, Wales or Scotland;
- (d) the objects of the company;
- (e) a statement that the liability of the members is to be limited;
- (f) the amount of the share capital with which the company proposes to be registered and the division thereof into shares of a fixed amount.

(ii) The Memorandum must be signed by each subscriber in the presence of at least one witness who must attest the signature. Each subscriber must take at least one share and must write opposite to his name the number of shares he takes.

(iii) The Memorandum of Association of a new public company must be in the form set out in Section 3 of the Companies Act 1985 or as near to that form as circumstances admit. Accordingly the address and description of each subscriber must be given and the Memorandum must be dated.

(iv) The Memorandum and Articles form the company's constitution and the Memorandum indicates the nature of the company's business, its capital and nationality. It must be stamped with the appropriate registration fee (see section 3.13 below).

(v) The name of a public company must end with the expression 'Public Limited Company', or the abbreviation 'P.L.C.'. In the case of a company with its registered office in Wales, the Welsh equivalent 'Cwmni Cyfyngedig Cyhoeddus' may be adopted, or the abbreviation 'C.C.C.'.

(vi) The share capital of a public company must be at least £50,000 as required by Section 11 of the Companies Act 1985.

(2) Articles of Association

On incorporation of a new public company, Articles may be registered with the Memorandum. All or any of the regulations contained in Table A (see Sections 7–8 of the Companies Act 1985) may be adopted. If Articles are not registered or, if Articles are registered, in so far as they do not exclude or modify the regulations in Table A, the Table A regulations will (so far as applicable) be the regulations of the company in the same manner and to the same extent as if they were contained in duly registered articles. Articles must be printed, divided into paragraphs and numbered consecutively. They must be signed by each subscriber to the Memorandum in the presence of at least one witness who must attest the signature.

---

(3) Statement of capital

This statement has to be given separately on Form No PUC1. Inland Revenue capital duty in respect of subscribers' shares taken on incorporation may be payable (see section 3.12 below).

---

(4) Statement of first directors and secretary and intended situation of registered office

The statement on Form No 10 must be delivered with the Memorandum.

---

(5) Declaration of compliance

A statutory declaration by a solicitor engaged in the formation of a company, or by a person named as director or secretary of the company in the statement on Form No 10 (see paragraph 3.1(4) above), that all the requirements of the Companies Act 1985 in respect of registration have been complied with must be produced to the Registrar (Form No 12).

A company registered as a public company must, before it commences business or exercises any borrowing powers, obtain the Registrar's certificate that it is entitled so to do.

3.2 Private Companies

The Companies Act (Section 1(3)(b)) states that a 'private company', unless the context otherwise requires, means a company that is not a public company. In other words, it cannot invite the public to subscribe for its shares.

The following documents must be delivered to the Registrar of Companies in connection with the registration of a private company.

(1) *Memorandum of Association*

(i) The Memorandum of Association of a private limited company must state the name of the company. It must also state the matters referred to in paragraphs 3.1(1)(i)(c), (d), (e) above. In the case of a private company limited by shares the statement referred to in paragraph 3.1(1)(i)(f) above must be included in the Memorandum. If the company is to be limited by guarantee the statement contained in Section 2(4) of the Companies Act 1985 must be included.

(ii) The Memorandum of a private company limited by shares and of a private company limited by guarantee must be in accordance with the forms set out in Tables B and C, respectively, of the Companies Regulations or as near as the circumstances admit.

(iii) The requirements as to signature of the Memorandum by subscribers and as to stamping with the appropriate registration fee are as described in paragraphs 3.1(1)(ii) and (iv) above.

(iv) The name of a private limited company must end with the word 'Limited' or the abbreviation 'Ltd'. In the case of a company with its registered office in Wales, the Welsh equivalent 'Cyfyngedig' or 'Cyf' may be used.

(2) Articles of Association

(i) The position with regard to the Articles of a private company limited by shares is set out in paragraph 3.1(2) above. Part II of Table A of the First Schedule to the Companies Act 1948, which contained regulations applicable in the case of a private company limited by shares, has been repealed. All or any of the regulations contained in Part I of Table A of the First Schedule of the Companies Act 1985 may be adopted.

(ii) A private company limited by guarantee must register Articles of Association. These must be in accordance with the form set out in Table C of the First Schedule to the Companies Act 1985, or as near thereto as circumstances admit. As with a public company, the Articles must be printed, divided into paragraphs, numbered consecutively and signed by each subscriber to the Memorandum in the presence of at least one witness who must attest to the signature. The addresses and descriptions of signatories must be given and the articles must be dated.

(3) Statement of capital (Form No PUC1)

A similar statement to that required for public companies must be given.

(4) Statement of first directors and secretary and intended situation of registered office (Form No 10)

The requirements are the same as for a public company; see paragraph 3.1(4) above.

(5) Declaration of compliance (Form No 12)
The same requirement as for a public company (paragraph 3.1(5) above). Under Section 12 of the Companies Act 1985, a private company is guilty of an offence if it:

(a) offers to the public (whether for cash or otherwise) any shares in or debentures of the company; or
(b) allots or agrees to allot (whether for cash or otherwise) any shares in or debentures of the company with a view to all or any of those shares or debentures being offered for sale to the public.

3.3 Companies with Registered Office in Wales

Section 2(2) of the Companies Act 1985 allows a company to state in its Memorandum of Association that its registered office is to be situated in 'Wales' rather than 'England'. A company that makes this statement in the Memorandum of Association may use the word 'Cyfyngedig' instead of 'Limited' in the last word of its name and deliver documents to the Registrar in Welsh. Documents submitted in Welsh should be accompanied by an English translation certified by:

(a) a notary public in England or Wales; or
(b) a solicitor of the Supreme Court.

3.4 Companies Not Having a Share Capital

The documents required are those prescribed for private companies, with the exception of the Statement of capital (Form No PUC1).

3.5 Overseas Companies

Companies incorporated outside Great Britain that have established a place of business inside Great Britain are obliged to register certain documents with the Registrar of Companies (see Chapter 6).

3.6 Name Protection

The registration of a name under company law does not provide protection against 'passing off' action under common law. Applicants are therefore advised in their own interest when applying for a company name to check with names already on the Register and if necessary seek legal advice.

3.7 Trade Marks

The Registrar does not consult the Trade Marks Index when considering applications for a proposed new company name, and the acceptance of a particular name is not an indication that no trade mark rights exist in it. Applicants are therefore advised in their own interests to avoid possible expense and inconvenience by investigating the possibility that others may have trade mark rights in the names – or parts of such names – they require before applying to the Registrar. Searches may be made at the Trade Marks Registry, Patent Office, 25 Southampton Buildings, London WC2A 1AY.

3.8 Consumer Credit Act

Registration of a company name should not be assumed to imply any subsequent acceptance of the same name for the purposes of the Consumer Credit Act 1974. Applicants who require a licence under the Consumer Credit Act 1974 in order to carry on their business are advised to consult the licensing branch of the Office of Fair Trading, Bromyard Avenue, Acton, London to ascertain whether the name is likely to be acceptable for the purposes of that Act.

3.9 Alien Directors

Some aliens are under restriction as to the employment in which they may engage while in the UK. If an alien director is in any doubt in this matter he should seek advice from the Home Office, Immigration and Nationality Department, Lunar House, Wellesley Road, Croydon, CR9 2BY (telephone: 01 686 0688).

3.10 Exchange Control Regulations

Companies having directors or shareholders who are resident outside the United Kingdom should bear in mind that monies may be transferred abroad only under the terms of Exchange Control Regulations (if there are any in force.)

3.11 Forms

Company forms can be obtained from law stationers, or from Companies Registration Office, Companies House, Crown Way, Maindy, Cardiff CF4 3UZ, the London Search Room, 55/71 City Road, London EC1Y 1BB (personal callers only) and, for Scotland, The Registrar of Companies, Exchequer Chambers, 102 George Street, Edinburgh EH2 3DJ.

3.12 Capital Duty

On the formation of a company incorporated with limited liability, duty (currently at £1 per £100 or part of £100) is charged on the greater of the nominal value of the shares issued or allotted on incorporation and the actual value of assets of any kind contributed less any liabilities that have been assumed or discharged by the company in consideration of the contribution.

3.13 Fees

A standard registration fee (currently £50) is payable irrespective of the amount of nominal capital, or the number of members in the case of a company without share capital.

3.14 Remittances

All remittances should be made payable to the Registrar of Companies and crossed 'A/c payee'.

Remittances in payment of Inland Revenue stamp duties in connection with new company registration may be sent, together with the registration fee, to the Registrar of Companies, who will arrange for the documents to be stamped by the Inland Revenue. Registrants may, however, get the documents stamped themselves by the Inland Revenue. Facilities are provided in London at the Inland Revenue Stamp Office, Bush House (SW wing), Strand, WC2R 1LB, and 61 Moorgate, EC2R 6BH, and elsewhere at the Inland Revenue Stamp Offices in Birmingham, Bristol, Cardiff, Edinburgh, Glasgow, Leeds, Liverpool, Manchester, Newcastle-upon-Tyne, Nottingham and Sheffield, where forms presented by an applicant can be denoted with Inland Revenue duty stamps on payment of the appropriate amount in cash.

3.15 The Obligation to Print Certain Documents (the Companies Act 1985; the European Communities Act, 1972)

You may have noticed on the preceding pages that you have an obligation to print certain documents. They are:

- Articles of Association
- altered Memorandums of Association
- altered Articles of Association.

The Registrar of Companies is prepared to regard the printing stipulation as satisfied by the following processes:

- letterpress, gravure, lithography

- stencil duplicating, using wax stencils and black ink, offset lithography, 'office' type-set

- electrostatic photocopying

- 'photostat' or similar processes properly processed and washed.

The following documents when submitted for registration must be either printed or in a form approved by the Registrar:

- ordinary resolutions increasing the capital of any company

- special and extraordinary resolutions and agreements as specified in Section 380 of the Companies Act 1985.

The Registrar is prepared to accept for registration such copy resolutions and agreements if produced by a process named above or if typed.

No document will be accepted if in general appearance, legibility, format or durability it is unsuitable for publication and use on the company's public file. It has been found by experience that documents produced by a semi-dry developed dye-line (diazo) system, by spirit duplicating or by thermo-copying do not satisfy the general conditions.

The Registrar's present practice is to accept copies of the Memorandum and Articles amended in accordance with the following rules:

(a) Where the amendment is small in extent, e.g. a change of name or a change in the nominal capital, a copy of the original document may be amended by rubber stamp, 'top copy' typing or in some other permanent manner (but not manuscript amendment).
(b) An alteration of a few lines or a complete short

paragraph may be similarly dealt with if the new version is satisfactorily permanently affixed to a copy of the original in such a way as to obscure the amended words.

(c) Where more substantial amendments are involved, the pages amended may be removed from a copy of the original, the amended text inserted and the pages securely collated. The inserted material must be 'printed' as defined above but need not be produced by the same process as the original.

In all cases the alterations must be validated by the seal or an official stamp of the company.

Where the document is produced other than by letterpress, a certificate by the printer stating the process used must be endorsed on or accompany the documents.

3.16 Summary of Regulations

- Two or more persons may form a private limited company.
- When applying for incorporation they must provide a **Memorandum of Association** and **Articles of Association** (in the business sense these two documents are usually referred to as the Mem & Arts).
- The Mem & Arts may be photocopied.
- They must choose a registered office.

- They will have to pay capital duty at the rate of £1 per £100 worth of shares.

- They need £50 registration fee.

3.17 Summary of Documents to be Submitted

(1) *Memorandum of Association:*	Private company limited by shares	Private company limited by guarantee	Private company unlimited liability	Public company
• Name of company must be shown	✓	✓	✓	✓
• Location of registered office must be shown	✓	✓	✓	✓
• Objects of the company must be shown	✓	✓	✓	✓
• Liability of members limited	✓	✓		✓
• Memorandum must be witnessed and signed by subscribers	✓	✓	✓	✓
• Name must end with 'Limited', 'Ltd' or Welsh equivalents	✓	✓		
• Share capital registered on incorporation must be shown	✓			✓
• Number of shares taken up by subscribers must be shown	✓			✓
• Memorandum must show that each member will contribute if company is wound up		✓		
• A public company must state that it is public				✓
• Share capital must be at least authorized minimum				✓
• Name must end in 'Public Limited Company', 'P.L.C.' or Welsh equivalent				✓

	Private company limited by shares	Private company limited by guarantee	Private company unlimited liability	Public company
(2) *Articles of Association:*				
• Articles must be printed	✓	✓	✓	✓
• Articles must have numbered consecutive paragraphs	✓	✓	✓	✓
• Articles must be witnessed and signed by subscriber	✓	✓	✓	✓
• Table in Companies Act 1985 to be followed	A	C	E	A
• Articles must be submitted by		✓	✓	
• Amount of share capital must be shown			✓	
(3) *Statement of Directors & registered office (Form No. 10):*				
• Must be submitted by	✓	✓	✓	✓
(4) *Declaration of compliance (Form No. 12):*				
• Must be submitted by	✓	✓	✓	✓
(5) *Statement of capital (PUC1):*				
• Must be submitted by	✓			✓

3.18 Enquiries about Registration

All enquiries relating to the registration of companies having their registered office in England and Wales should be addressed to the Registrar of Companies, Companies House, Crown Way, Maindy, Cardiff CF4 3UZ (Tel: 0222 388588). Companies records in microfiche form can be inspected at the above address and at the London Search Room, Companies House, 55–71 City Road, London EC1Y 1BB (Tel: 01 253 9393).

Enquiries relating to companies having their registered office in Scotland should be addressed to the Registrar of Companies, 102 George Street, Edinburgh EH2 3DJ (Tel: 031 225 5774/5).

Northern Ireland operates its own independent Companies Acts and all enquiries about companies registered there should be addressed to the Registrar of Companies, Department of Commerce, 43–47 Chichester Street, Belfast BT1 4RJ (Tel: Belfast 34121).

3.19 Delivery of Documents to the Registrar

Documents required to be delivered to the Registrar can be delivered by hand to either Cardiff or London in the case of companies with their registered office in England or Wales, and to Edinburgh in the case of companies having their registered office in Scotland.

3.20 Specimen Documents

Let us now look in detail at the various documents that must be sent to the Companies Registration Office.

Forms No PUC1, No 10 and No 12
On pages 42–48 you will first find a specimen letter of

application for the necessary free forms, followed by specimens of the forms, which you can adapt to your own company. Do not sign Form No 12 until you are in the presence of a Commissioner of Oaths.

Memorandum of Association

This part of the formation package must be signed by at least two persons, each having a minimum of one share. It contains five main clauses:

(1) The company name.
(2) Its registered office.
(3) The objects clause. This gives the nature of the business. You will find it best to have an objects clause covering almost any conceivable business enterprise. For this reason I have included a specimen Memorandum (pp. 49–57) that is far-reaching in its objects.
(4) The fact that it is a limited company.
(5) The share capital.

Important

A fact that is not known to many! A director of a company can incur personal liability if he engages in a business that is not mentioned by the objects clause.

Articles of Association

This document contains the internal regulations of the company. It is also signed by at least two persons. The specimen Articles (pp. 58–62) are satisfactory for the majority of companies as they contain the rules governing the management of the company such as the control of shares, general meetings and directors' powers.

SPECIMEN LETTER

27 Atlantic House
Stratford on Avon

Date

Companies Registration Office
Appropriate Companies House

Sir,
I am in the process of forming a Limited Company. Please supply the following forms:

Nos PUC1, 10 and 12.

I look forward to receiving them {as soon as possible. / at your earliest convenience.}

Yours faithfully,

J. DANIELS

Form No. PUC1 (revised)

G

Statement on formation of a company to be incorporated with limited liability under the Companies Act 1948

Pursuant to Part V of the Finance Act 1973

Please do not write in this binding margin

Please complete legibly, preferably in black type, or bold block lettering

For official use | Company number

Please do not write in the space below. For Inland Revenue use only

Name of company

THE BUSINESS BOOK CLUB Limited*

*delete if inappropriate

†Distinguish between ordinary, preference, etc.

A Nominal Capital	£ 100		
Description of shares†	Ordinary		
B Nominal value of each share	£ 1	£	£
C Number of shares taken on incorporation	2		
D Total amount payable on each (including premium if any)	£ 1	£	£
E Amount paid or due and payable on each	£ 1	£	£
F Total amount paid or due and payable in respect of C	£ 2		
G Capital duty payable on F at £1 per £100 or part of £100	£ 1		

Notes

This form must be delivered to the Registrar of Companies when applying for incorporation of the company.

If amounts are contributed otherwise than in cash, that fact with full particulars must be stated and attached to this form. ☐ Please tick box if attached

I hereby certify that the above particulars are correct in all respects

‡delete as appropriate

Signed BY HILARY EVANS [~~Director~~] [Secretary]‡ Date 21 JULY 19

Presentor's name, address and reference (if any):

J. DANIELS
27 ATLANTIC AVE
STRATFORD ON AVON

For official use
Capital section | Post room

COMPANIES FORM No. 10

Statement of first directors and secretary and intended situation of registered office

10

Please do not write in this margin

Pursuant to section 10 of the Companies Act 1985

To the Registrar of Companies

For official use

Please complete legibly, preferably in black type, or bold block lettering

Name of company

* insert full name of company

* THE BUSINESS BOOK CLUB LIMITED

The intended situation of the registered office of the company on incorporation is as stated below

27 ATLANTIC AVENUE
STRATFORD ON AVON

Postcode

If the memorandum is delivered by an agent for the subscribers of the memorandum please mark 'X'in the box opposite and insert the agent's name and address below

Postcode

Number of continuation sheets attached (see note 1)

Presentor's name address and reference (if any):

J. DANIELS
27 ATLANTIC AVE
STRATFORD ON AVON

For official Use
General Section
Post room

The name(s) and particulars of the person who is, or the persons who are, to be the first director or directors of the company (note 2) are as follows:

Please do not write in this margin

Name (note 3) JACK DANIELS	Business occupation BOOK SALESMAN
Previous name(s) (note 3)	Nationality BRITISH
Address (note 4) 27 ATLANTIC AVENUE STRATFORD ON AVON	Date of birth (where applicable) (note 6)
Postcode	
Other directorships † NONE	
I consent to act as director of the company named on page 1	
Signature OF J. DANIELS	Date 21 JULY 19

† enter particulars of other directorships held or previously held (see note 5) if this space is insufficient use a continuation sheet.

Name (note 3)	Business occupation
Previous name(s) (note 3)	Nationality
Address (note 4)	Date of birth (where applicable) (note 6)
Postcode	
Other directorships †	
I consent to act as director of the company named on page 1	
Signature	Date

Name (note 3)	Business occupation
Previous name(s) (note 3)	Nationality
Address (note 4)	Date of birth (where applicable) (note 6)
Postcode	
Other directorships †	
I consent to act as director of the company named on page 1	
Signature	Date

Please do not write in this margin

Please complete legibly, preferably in black type, or bold block lettering

The name(s) and particulars of the person who is, or the persons who are,to be the first secretary, or joint secretaries, of the company are as follows:

Name (notes 3 & 7) HILARY EVANS

Previous name(s) (note 3) NEE RUSSELL

Address (notes 4 & 7) 45 STRATFORD ROAD

OFFENHAM

Postcode

I consent to act as secretary of the company named on page 1

Signature OF HILARY EVANS Date 21 JULY 19

Name (notes 3 & 7)

Previous name(s) (note 3)

Address (notes 4 & 7)

Postcode

I consent to act as secretary of the company named on page 1

Signature Date

delete if the form is signed by the subcribers

Signature of agent on behalf of subsribers Date

delete if the form is signed by an agent on behalf of the subscribers.

All the subscribers must sign either personally or by a person or persons authorised to sign for them.

Signed	BY JACK DANIELS	Date	21 JULY 19
Signed	BY HILARY EVANS	Date	21 JULY 19
Signed		Date	
Signed		Date	
Signed		Date	
Signed		Date	

Notes

1 If the spaces on Page 2 are insufficient the names and particulars must be entered on the prescribed continuation sheet(s).

2 'Director' includes any person who occupies the position of a director, by whatever name called.

3. For an individual, his present christian name(s) and surname must be given, together with any previous christian name(s) or surname(s).

"Christian name" includes a forename. In the case of a peer or person usually known by a title different from his surname, "surname" means that title. In the case of a corporation, its corporate name must be given.

A previous christian name or surname need not be given if:—

(a) in the case of a married woman, it was a name by which she was known before her marriage; or

(b) it was changed or ceased to be used at least 20 years ago, or before the person who previously used it reached the age of 18; or

(c) in the case of a peer or a person usually known by a British title different from his surname, it was a name by which he was known before he adopted the title or succeeded to it

4 Usual residential address must be given or, in the case of a corporation, the registered or principal office.

5 The names must be given of all bodies corporate incorporated in Great Britain of which the director is also a director, or has been a director at any time during the preceeding five years.

However, a present or past directorship need not be disclosed if it is, or has been, held in a body corporate which, throughout that directorship, has been:—

(a) a dormant company (which is a company which has had no transactions required to be entered in the company's accounting records, except any which may have arisen from the taking of shares in the company by a subscriber to the memorandum as such).

(b) a body corporate of which the company making the return was a wholly-owned subsidiary;

(c) a wholly-owned subsidiary of the company making the return; or

(d) a wholly-owned subsidiary of a body corporate of which the company making the return was also a wholly owned subsidiary.

6. Dates of birth need only be given if the company making the return is:—

(a) a public company;
(b) the subsidiary of a public company; or
(c) the subsidiary of a public company registered in Northern Ireland

7 Where all the partners in a firm are joint secretaries, only the name and principal office of the firm need be stated.

Where the secretary or one of the joint secretaries is a Scottish firm the details required are the firm name and its principal office.

COMPANIES FORM No. 12

Statutory Declaration of compliance with requirements on application for registration of a company

12

Please do not write in this margin

Pursuant to section 12(3) of the Companies Act 1985

Please complete legibly, preferably in black type, or bold block lettering

To the Registrar of Companies

For official use

For official use

Name of company

* insert full name of Company

* THE BUSINESS BOOK CLUB LIMITED

I, JACK DANIELS

of 27 ATLANTIC AVE, STRATFORD ON AVON

† delete as appropriate

do solemnly and sincerely declare that I am a [person named as director or secretary of the company in the statement delivered to the registrar under section 10(2)]† and that all the requirements of the above Act in respect of the registration of the above company and of matters precedent and incidental to it have been complied with,

And I make this solemn declaration conscientiously believing the same to be true and by virtue of the provisions of the Statutory Declarations Act 1835

Declared at ______

the ______ day of ______

One thousand nine hundred and ______

before me ______

A Commissioner for Oaths or Notary Public or Justice of the Peace or Solicitor having the powers conferred on a Commissioner for Oaths.

Declarant to sign below

ONLY SIGN IN FRONT OF A COMMISSIONER FOR OATHS

Presentor's name address and reference (if any):

J. DANIELS
27 ATLANTIC AVE
STRATFORD ON AVON

For official Use New Companies Section	Post room

THE COMPANIES ACT 1985

COMPANY LIMITED BY SHARES

MEMORANDUM OF ASSOCIATION

OF

THE BUSINESS BOOK CLUB LIMITED

1. The Name of the Company is THE BUSINESS BOOK CLUB LIMITED
2. The Registered Office of the Company will be situate in England.
3. The Objects for which the Company is established are:—

(A) To carry on all or any of the businesses of general merchants and traders, manufacturers, assemblers, distributors, importers, exporters, merchants, factors and shippers of and wholesale and retail dealers in goods, wares, produce, products, commodities, fancy goods, handicrafts, and merchandise of every description, to act as agents for and to enter into agreements and arrangements of all kinds on behalf of such persons, firms or companies as may be thought expedient, and to negotiate, assign and mortgage or pledge for cash or otherwise, any such agreements and the payments due thereunder and any property the subject thereof, to carry on all or any of the businesses of mail order specialists, credit and discount traders, cash and carry traders, manufacturers' agents, commission and general agents, brokers, factors, warehousemen, and agents in respect of raw and manufactured goods, of all kinds, and general railway, shipping and forwarding agents and transport contractors; to create, establish, build up, and maintain an organisation for the marketing, selling, retailing, servicing, advertisement,distribution or introduction of the products, merchandise, goods, wares, and commodities dealt in or services rendered by any persons, firms or companies, and to participate in, undertake, perform, and carry out all kinds of commercial, trading and financial operations and all or any of the operations ordinarily performed by import, export and general merchants, factors, shippers, agents, traders, distributors, capitalists, and financiers, either on the Company's own account or otherwise; and to open and establish shops, stalls, stores, markets and depots for the sale, collection and distribution of the goods dealt in by the Company.

(B) To carry on any other trade or business which may seem to the Company capable of being conveniently carried on in connection with the objects specified in Sub-Clause (A) hereof or calculated directly or indirectly to enhance the value of or render profitable any of the property or rights of the Company.

(C) To purchase, take on lease or in exchange, hire or otherwise acquire and hold for any estate or interest any lands, buildings, easements, rights, privileges, concessions, patents, patent rights, licences, secret processes, machinery, plant, stock-in-trade, and any real or personal property of any kind necessary or convenient for the purposes of or in connection with the Company's business or any branch or department thereof.

(D) To erect, construct, lay down, enlarge, alter and maintain any roads, railways, tramways, sidings, bridges, reservoirs, shops, stores, factories, buildings, works, plant and machinery necessary or convenient for the Company's business, and to contribute to or subsidise the erection, construction and maintenance of any of the above.

(E) To borrow or raise or secure the payment of money in such manner as the Company shall think fit for the purposes of or in connection with the Company's business, and for the purposes of or in connection with the borrowing or raising of money by the Company to become a member of any building society.

(F) For the purposes of or in connection with the business of the Company to mortgage and charge the undertaking and all or any of the real and personal property and assets, present and future, and all or any of the uncalled capital for the time being of the Company, and to issue at par or at a premium or discount, and for such consideration and with and subject to such rights, powers, privileges and conditions as may be thought fit, debentures or debenture stock, either permanent or redeemable or repayable, and collaterally or further to secure any securities of the Company by a trust deed or other assurances. To issue and deposit any securities which the Company has power to issue by way of mortgage to secure any sum less than the nominal amount of such securities, and also by way of security for the performance of any contracts or obligations of the Company or of its customers or other persons or corporations having dealings with the Company, or in whose businesses or undertakings the Company is interested, whether directly or indirectly.

(G) To receive money on deposit or loan upon such terms as the Company may approve.

(H) To lend money to any company, firm or person and to give all kinds of indemnities and either with or without the Company receiving any consideration or advantage, direct or indirect, for giving any such guarantee, and whether or not such guarantee is given in connection with or pursuant to the attainment of the objects herein stated to guarantee either by personal covenant or by mortgaging or charging all or any part of the undertaking, property and assets present and future and uncalled capital of the Company or by both such methods, the performance of the obligations and the payment of the capital or principal (together with any premium) of and dividends or interest on any debenture, stocks, shares or other securities of any company, firm or person and in particular (but without limiting the generality of the foregoing) any company which is for the time being the Company's Holding or Subsidiary company as defined by Sections 736 and 744 of the Companies Act, 1985, or otherwise associated with the Company in business.

(l) To establish and maintain or procure the establishment and maintenance of any non-contributory or contributory pension or superannuation funds for the benefit of, and give or procure the giving of donations, gratuities, pensions, allowances, or emoluments to any persons who are or were at any time in the employment or service of the Company, or of any company which is for the time being the Company's Holding or Subsidiary company as defined by Sections 736 and 744 of the Companies Act, 1985, or otherwise associated with the Company in business or who are or were at any time Directors or officers of the Company or of any such other company as aforesaid, and the wives, widows, families and dependents of any such persons, and also to establish and subsidise or subscribe to any institutions, associations, clubs or funds calculated to be for the benefit of or to advance the interests and well-being of the Company or of any such other company as aforesaid, or of any such persons as aforesaid, and to make payments for or towards the insurance of any such persons as aforesaid, and to subscribe or guarantee money for charitable or benevolent objects or for any exhibition or for any public, general or useful object, and to do any of the matters aforesaid either alone or in conjunction with any such other company as aforesaid.

(J) To draw, make, accept, endorse, negotiate, discount and execute promissory notes, bills of exchange and other negotiable instruments.

(K) To invest and deal with the moneys of the Company not immediately required for the purposes of its business in or upon such investments or securities and in such manner as may from time to time be determined.

(L) To pay for any property or rights acquired by the Company, either in cash or fully or partly paid-up shares, with or without preferred or deferred or special rights or restrictions in respect of dividend, repayment of capital voting or otherwise, or by any securities which the Company has power to issue, or partly in one mode and partly in another, and generally on such terms as the Company may determine.

(M) To accept payment for any property or rights sold or otherwise disposed of or dealt with by the Company, either in cash, by instalments or otherwise, or in fully or partly paid-up shares of any company or corporation, with or without deferred or preferred or special rights or restrictions in respect of dividend, repayment of capital, voting or otherwise, or in debentures or mortgage debentures or debenture stock, mortgages or other securities of any company or corporation, or partly in one mode and partly in another, and generally on such terms as the Company may determine, and to hold, dispose of or otherwise deal with any shares, stock or securities so acquired.

(N) To enter into any partnership or joint-purse arrangement or arrangement for sharing profits, union of interests or co-operation with any company, firm or person carrying on or proposing to carry on any business within the objects of this Company, and to acquire and hold, sell, deal with or dispose of shares, stock or securities of any such company, and to guarantee the contracts or liabilities of, or the payment of the dividends, interest or capital of any shares, stock or securities of and to subsidise or otherwise assist any such company.

(O) To establish or promote or concur in establishing or promoting any other company whose objects shall include the acquisition and taking over of all or any of the assets and liabilities of this Company or the promotion of which shall be in any manner calculated to advance directly or indirectly the objects or interests of this Company, and to acquire and hold or dispose of shares, stock or securities and guarantee the payment of dividends, interest or capital of any shares, stock or securities issued by or any other obligations of any such company.

(P) To purchase or otherwise acquire and undertake all or any part of the business, property, assets, liabilities and transactions of any person, firm or company carrying on any business which this Company is authorised to carry on or possessed of property suitable for the purposes of the Company, or which can be carried on in conjunction therewith or which is capable of being conducted so as directly or indirectly to benefit the Company.

(Q) To sell, improve, manage, develop, turn to account, exchange, let on rent, grant royalty, share of profits or otherwise, grant licences, easements and other rights in or over, and in any other manner deal with or dispose of the undertaking and all or any of the property and assets for the time being of the Company for such consideration as the Company may think fit.

(R) To amalgamate with any other company whose objects are or include objects similar to those of this Company, whether by sale or purchase (for fully or partly paid-up shares or otherwise) of the undertaking, subject to the liabilities of this or any such other company as aforesaid, with or without winding up, or by sale or purchase (for fully or partly paid-up shares or otherwise) of all or a controlling interest in the shares or stock of this or any such other company as aforesaid, or by partnership, or any arrangement of the nature of partnership, or in any other manner.

(S) To subscribe for, purchase or otherwise acquire, and hold shares, stock, debentures or other securities of any other company.

(T) To distribute among the members in specie any property of the Company, or any proceeds of sale or disposal of any property of the Company, but so that no distribution amounting to a reduction of capital be made except with the sanction (if any) for the time being required by law.

(U) To do all or any of the above things in any part of the world, and either as principals, agents, trustees, contractors or otherwise, and either alone or in conjunction with others, and either by or through agents, trustees, sub-contractors or otherwise.

(V) To do all such things as are incidental or conducive to the above objects or any of them.

And it is hereby declared that, save as otherwise expressly provided, each of the paragraphs of this Clause shall be regarded as specifying separate and independent objects and accordingly shall not be in anywise limited by reference to or inference from any other paragraph or the name of the Company and the provisions of each such paragraph shall, save as aforesaid, be carried out in as full and ample a manner and construed in as wide a sense as if each of the paragraphs defined the objects of a separate and distinct company.

4. The liability of the Members is limited.

5. The share capital of the Company is £100 divided into 100 shares of £1 each.

WE, the several persons whose Names, Addresses and Descriptions are subscribed, are desirous of being formed into a Company, in pursuance of this Memorandum of Association, and we respectively agree to take the number of Shares in the Capital of the Company set opposite our respective names.

NAMES, ADDRESSES AND DESCRIPTIONS OF SUBSCRIBERS	Number of Shares taken by each Subscriber
JACK DANIELS 27 ATLANTIC AVE STRATFORD ON AVON SIGNATURE OF ABOVE BOOKSELLER	ONE
HILARY EVANS 45 STRATFORD ROAD OFFENHAM SIGNATURE OF ABOVE SALES CLERK	ONE

Dated the day of 19

Witness to the above Signatures:–

AMY DANIELS' SIGNATURE

AMY DANIELS
27 ATLANTIC AVE
STRATFORD ON AVON

HOUSEWIFE

The Companies Act 1985

COMPANY LIMITED BY SHARES

Articles of Association

OF

THE BUSINESS BOOK CLUB

LIMITED

---

1. Subject as hereinafter provided, the regulations contained in Table A in The Companies (Tables A to F) Regulations 1985 (hereinafter referred to as "Table A") shall apply to the Company.

2. Regulations 8, 64, 76, 77 and 113 of Table A shall not apply to the Company.

3. The Company is a private company and accordingly no offer or invitation shall be made to the public (whether for cash or otherwise) to subscribe for any shares in or debentures of the Company, nor shall the Company allot or agree to allot (whether for cash or otherwise) any shares in or debentures of the Company with a view to all or any of those shares or debentures being offered for sale to the public.

4. At the date of the adoption of these Articles the capital of the Company is £100 divided into 100 Ordinary Shares of £1 each.

---

5. (a) The Directors may subject to Article 6 hereof allot, grant options over, or otherwise deal with or dispose of any relevant securities (as defined by section 80(2) of the Companies Act 1985) of the Company to such persons and generally on such terms and conditions as the Directors think proper.

(b) The general authority conferred by paragraph (a) of this Article shall be conditional upon due compliance with Article 6 hereof and shall extend to the amount of the authorised share capital of the Company upon its incorporation. The said authority will expire on 19 unless renewed, varied or revoked by the Company in general meeting in accordance with the said section 80.

(c) The Directors shall be entitled under the general authority conferred by paragraph (a) of this Article to make at any time before the expiry of such authority any offer or agreement which will or might require relevant securities of the Company to be allotted after the expiry of such authority.

6. (a) Subject to any direction to the contrary that may be given by the Company in general meeting all shares authorised pursuant to Article 5 hereof to be allotted shall be offered to the members in proportion to the existing shares held by them and such offer shall be made by notice in writing specifying the number of the shares to which the member is entitled and limiting a time (being not less than 21 days) within which the offer if not accepted will be deemed to have been declined, and after the expiry of such time or upon receipt of an intimation from the member to whom such notice is given that he declines to accept the shares offered, the Directors may, subject to these Articles, allot or otherwise dispose of the same to such persons and upon such terms as they think most beneficial to the Company. The Directors may in like manner dispose of any such shares as aforesaid which, by reason of the proportion borne by them to the number of persons entitled to any such offer as aforesaid or by reason of any other difficulty in apportioning the same,

cannot in the opinion of the Directors be conveniently offered in manner hereinbefore provided.

(b) By virtue of section 91(1) of the Companies Act 1985, sections 89(1) and 90(1) to 90(6) inclusive of that Act shall not apply to the Company.

7. The Company shall have a first and paramount lien on every share (whether or not it is a fully paid share) for all moneys (whether presently payable or not) called or payable at a fixed time in respect of that share and the Company shall also have a first and paramount lien on all shares (whether fully paid or not) standing registered in the name of any member whether solely or one of two or more joint holders for all moneys presently payable by him or his estate to the Company; but the Directors may at any time declare any share to be wholly or in part exempt from the provisions of this Article. The Company's lien (if any) on a share shall extend to all dividends payable thereon.

8. The Directors may, in their absolute discretion and without assigning any reason therefore, decline to register any transfer of any share, whether or not it is a fully paid share. The first sentence of regulation 24 of Table A shall not apply to the Company.

9. In accordance with section 372(3) of the Companies Act 1985 in every notice calling a General Meeting of the Company there shall appear with reasonable prominence a statement that a member entitled to attend and vote is entitled to appoint a proxy to attend and vote instead of him and that a proxy need not be a member of the Company. Regulation 38 of Table A shall be modified accordingly and the second sentence of Regulation 59 of Table A shall not apply to the Company.

10. In regulation 41 of Table A there shall be added at the end: "If at any adjourned meeting a quorum is not present

within half an hour from the time appointed for the meeting the meeting shall be dissolved."

11. Unless and until the Company in general meeting shall otherwise determine, there shall be no maximum number of Directors and the minimum number of Directors shall be one. If and so long as there is a sole Director he may exercise all the powers and authorities vested in the Directors by these Articles and by Table A and regulation 89 of Table A shall be modified accordingly. The first Directors of the Company shall be as named in the statement delivered to the Registrar of Companies pursuant to section 10 of the Companies Act 1985.

12. The Company shall not be subject to section 293 of the Companies Act 1985, and accordingly any person may be appointed or elected as a Director, whatever his age, and no Director shall be required to vacate his office of Director by reason of his attaining or having attained the age of seventy years or any other age.

13. No person other than a Director retiring by rotation shall be elected a Director at any general meeting unless—

(i) he is recommended by the Directors; or

(ii) not less than fourteen or more than thirty-five clear days before the date of the meeting a notice in writing signed by a member qualified to vote at the meeting has been given to the Company of the intention to propose that person for election, together with a notice in writing signed by that person of his willingness to be elected.

14. A Director shall not be required to hold any share qualification but shall nevertheless be entitled to receive notice of and to attend at all general meetings of the Company and at all separate general meetings of the holders of any class of shares in the capital of the Company.

NAMES, ADDRESSES AND DESCRIPTIONS OF SUBSCRIBERS

JACK DANIELS
27 ATLANTIC AVE
STRATFORD ON AVON
SIGNATURE OF ABOVE

BOOK SELLER

HILARY EVANS
45 STRATFORD ROAD
OFFENHAM
SIGNATURE OF ABOVE

SALES CLERK

DATED THE DAY OF 19
Witness to the above Signatures:–

AMY DANIELS — AMY DANIELS' SIGNATURE
27 ATLANTIC AVE
STRATFORD ON AVON

HOUSEWIFE

3.21 Summary of Application Procedure

- You've completed Form No PUC1.
- You've completed Form No 10.
- You've completed Form No 12 **(DON'T SIGN YET).**
- You've completed the Mem & Arts.
- You take all those documents to a Commissioner for Oaths who charges you about £2 to attest your signature on Form No 12.
- You photocopy the paperwork for your records.
- You make out a cheque for £50 payable to Registrar of Companies and crossed A/c payee.
- You send off to Companies House: Form Nos PUC1, 10 and 12, Mem & Arts and £50.
- With a sense of satisfaction you sit back and wait for your Certificate of Incorporation.

4

Arrival of Certificate of Incorporation

Once the Memorandum has been registered, legal formalities completed and fees paid, your Certificate of Incorporation arrives (amongst other things) in an envelope marked 'Do Not Bend' to enable you to have a non-creased document to frame if you wish. This certificate must be displayed in your business premises. (A specimen copy is reproduced on p. 65)

From the date of the Certificate of Incorporation the subscribers to the Memorandum (and shareholders) become a legal entity (body corporate) and can now commence trading, open a bank account, own property, borrow money and employ labour. With your certificate you usually receive:

- *Notes for the Guidance of Registered Companies* (which have been covered in this book), plus a list of forms that may be needed during the life of your corporation.
- *Should I be registered for VAT?* A useful booklet for the new company, which covers the whys and wherefores of VAT and the starting amounts (presently £19,500).

CERTIFICATE OF INCORPORATION

OF A PRIVATE LIMITED COMPANY

No.

I hereby certify that

is this day incorporated under the Companies Act 1985 as a private company and that the Company is limited.

Given under my hand at the Companies Registration Office, Cardiff the

an authorised officer

C.173

- A letter explaining that you must pay attention to the need to deliver certain documents – e.g. annual returns and accounts, notification of change of directors and secretaries or registered office – and the need for you to register promptly any mortgage or charge taken out by the company.

- Form No 224 (Notice of accounts reference date), to be completed and returned to the CRO within six months of the date of incorporation shown on the certificate.

Alright – what do we do now?

4.1 Supplies

It was inadvisable to incur expense until the company was incorporated, but now you will need business stationery, a company seal, a register and a company sign. I found in my research that 'company formations' specialists, solicitors and accountants charge an average £29 for both seal and register. Individually I found the seal cost £15 (+VAT and post and package) and the register £20–25. Prices can be higher, but then you have the highest-quality goods with gold blocking and the like.

The idea of this book is to help an individual form a company at the lowest possible cost. For this reason I can personally recommend the following company:

Corporate Services
15 Borough High Street
London S.E.1.

Their prices are very competitive and they have been

recommended for their service and reliability. They provide a company seal and company ledger for an all-in price of £25 (includes VAT and post and packing). They can also provide name plates, forms, registered office facilities and other matters relating to companies. I suggest you write first for up-to-date prices.

4.2 Copies of Mem & Arts

You will need photocopies of the Mem & Arts for the bank, solicitor, accountant, directors and office copy (8 copies is the usual). Prior to the photocopying of your Mem & Arts, I suggest you create a cover for them in the manner shown:

COMPANY NUMBER

THE COMPANIES ACT 1985

COMPANY LIMITED BY SHARES

MEMORANDUM AND
ARTICLES OF ASSOCIATION OF

____

Incorporated the day of 19

You will then have a permanent record of your company details on your Mem & Arts.

4.3 Opening a Bank Account

Your bank will need one copy of your Mem & Arts (which they will hold in their files) and sight of the Certificate of Incorporation before they will open a bank account in the company name.

4.4 The First Meeting of the Company

You will find specimen minutes on p. 69. These can be added to as you see the need. Once the shares have been allocated you must send off Form No PUC2 (see specimen on p. 70).

Minutes of the first meeting of the company

THE BUSINESS BOOK CLUB LTD

The first meeting of the company was held at ______ in the City of ______ on the ______ day of ______ 19__ at ______ o'clock.

Present – JACK DANIELS AND HILARY EVANS

The Certificate of Incorporation was produced.

The seal, an impression of which was made in the margin hereof, was duly approved and adopted as the seal of the company.

It was resolved that Jack Daniels and Hilary Evans be appointed the first directors and that Jack Daniels be appointed the chairman of the company.

It was resolved that Hilary Daniels be appointed secretary of the company in accordance with the Articles of Association.

It was resolved that the registered office of the company be at

______

Shares were allocated to J. Daniels (1) and H. Evans (1) and recorded in the Applications and Allotments section of the register.

Form No. PUC2 was prepared, signed and sent to the ROC with the capital duty of £1.

There being no further business before the meeting it was adjourned.

______

Chairman

______

Secretary

Form No. PUC2

Return of allotments of shares issued for cash

PUC2

Pursuant to section 88(2) of the Companies Act 1985
and Part V of the Finance Act 1973

Please do not write in this margin

Please complete legibly, preferably in black type, or bold block lettering

For official use

Company number

Your registration number

Please do not write in the space below. For inland Revenue use only

Name of company

* insert full name of company

* THE BUSINESS BOOK CLUB LIMITED

† distinguish between ordinary, preference, etc.

Description of shares†	ordinary		
A Number allotted	2		
B Nominal value of each	£ 1	£	£
C Total amount payable on each share (including premium if any)	£ 1	£	£
D Amount paid or due and payable on each share. (Take into account premium if any or part payments made)	£ 1	£	£
E Total amount paid or due and payable (A×D)	£ 2		
F Capital duty payable on E at £1 per £100 or part of £100§	£ 1		

§ you are reminded of the fine(s) imposed on a company by virtue of section 47(7) of the Finance Act 1973 if the relative duty is not paid within one month of allotments

ø delete or complete as appropriate

Date(s) of allotment(s)

[made on the 21 JULY 19 ____]ø

[from the ____ 19 ____ to the ____ 19 ____]ø

The names, and addresses of the allottees should be given overleaf

If you are claiming credit or relief from capital duty under section 49(5) of the Finance Act 1973 a Form No. PUC4 must be completed and attached to this form.

If you are claiming relief from capital duty under paragraph 9 of Schedule 19 of the Finance Act 1973 or section 161 of the Companies Act 1985, a letter to that effect should accompany this form.

Please tick box if attached

This form should not be used for shares allotted by way of bonus — Form No. 88(2) should be used instead.

Presentor's name address and reference (if any):

J. DANIELS
27 ATLANTIC AVENUE
STRATFORD ON AVON

For official Use

Capital Section

Post room

Names, descriptions and addresses of the allottees

Please do not write in this binding margin.

Please complete legibly, preferably in black type, or bold block lettering

Name and description	Address	Number of shares allotted		
		Preference	Ordinary	Other kinds
J. DANIELS	27 ATLANTIC AVENUE			
	STRATFORD ON AVON		1	
H. EVANS	45 STRATFORD ROAD			
	OFFENHAM		1	
	Total		2	

Where the space given on this form is inadequate, continuation sheets should be used and the number of sheets attached should be indicated in the box opposite:

I hereby certify that the details entered on this form are correct.

Signed of J.Daniels [Director] [Secretary]‡ Date 21 JULY 19

‡delete as appropriate

Page 2

4.5 The Company Register

This can be purchased (see section 4.1) or, to keep expenses down, you could start with a combined loose-leaf binder to keep your records. It should contain:

- applications and allotments
- transfers
- mortgages
- debentures
- members
- directors and secretaries
- directors' interests
- annual list of members, directors and secretaries
- minutes
- share certificate

On pages 73–83 you will find specimens of each.

APPLICATIONS AND ALLOTMENTS

Date of Application	NAME, ADDRESS AND OCCUPATION	No. of Shares Applied For	Amount of Deposit	SHARES ALLOTTED					Further Amount Payable	Amount Returnable	Folio in Register of Members	REMARKS
				Allot-ment No.	No. of Shares Allotted	Distinctive Numbers (inclusive)		Issue Price				
						From	To					

REGISTER OF TRANSFERS

Date	Number of Transfer	TRANSFERORS			TRANSFEREES			Number of Shares Transferred	Distinctive Numbers of Shares Transferred		Transfer Value
		Folio in Register of Members	NAME	Address and Occupation	NAME	Address and Occupation	Folio in Register of Members		From	To	

PARTICULARS OF A MORTGAGE OR CHARGE

Date and Description of the Instrument Creating or Evidencing the Mortgage or Charge and Description thereof. (A description of the Instrument—*e.g.* Trust Deed, Mortgage, &c., as the case may be—should be given.)	Amount secured by the Mortgage or Charge	Short Particulars of the Property Mortgaged or Charged	Names (with Addresses and Descriptions) of the Mortgagees, or Persons Entitled to the Charge	Amount or rate per cent of the Commission, Allowance, or Discount (if any) paid or made either directly or indirectly by the Company to any person in consideration of his subscribing or agreeing to subscribe, whether absolutely or conditionally, or procuring or agreeing to procure subscriptions, whether absolute or conditional, for any of the Debentures included in this return.

REGISTER OF DEBENTURES

Date of Debenture	No. of Debenture	Amount	Name and Address of Debenture Holder	Description of Property Charged	INTEREST				REMARKS
					Rate per Annum	Amount before deducting Income Tax		Date or Dates becoming Due	
						Per Annum	Per Instalment		

REGISTER OF MEMBERS AND SHARE LEDGER

Name   Date of Entry as a Member   19

Address   Date of Ceasing to be a Member   19

SHARES ACQUIRED							Dr.	ALLOTMENT CASH ACCOUNT					SHARES TRANSFERRED						Cr.
Date of Acquisition by Allotment or Transfer	Allot-ment No.	Transfer No.	Folio in Register of Allotments or Register of Transfers	No. of Shares acquired by Allotment or Transfer	Distinctive Numbers (inclusive)		NOMINAL VALUE OF SHARES ACQUIRED	Payable on Shares Allotted		Paid or Agreed to be Considered as Paid			Date of Transfer	Transfer No.	Folio in Register of Transfers	Number of Shares Trans-ferred	Distinctive Numbers (inclusive)		NOMINAL VALUE OF SHARES TRANSFERRED
					From	To		Amount per Share	Total Amount Dr.	Date	Folio	Amount Cr.					From	To	

REGISTER OF DIRECTORS* AND SECRETARIES

(Columns 5, 7 and 8 need not be completed in the case of a Secretary)

1	2	3	4	5	6	7	8	9	
Date of Appointment	Nature of Appointment (i.e. whether Director or Secretary)	Name (In the case of an individual, present Christian† name or names and surname. In the case of a corporation, the corporate name.)**	Any former Christian name or names and surname‡	Nationality	Usual residential address. (In the case of a corporation, the registered or principal office.)	Business occupation and particulars of other directorships§	Date of Birth	Changes	
								Date of change	Nature of Change

NOTES

* "Director" includes any person who occupies the position of a Director by whatsoever name called, and any person in accordance with whose directions or instructions the directors of the company are accustomed to act.

† "Christian name" includes a forename, and "surname" in the case of a peer or person usually known by a title different from his surname, means that title.

‡ "Former Christian name" and "former surname" do not include—

(*a*) In the case of a peer or a person usually known by a British title different from his surname, the name by which he was known previous to the adoption of or succession to the title; or

(*b*) In the case of any person, a former Christian name or surname where that name or surname was changed or disused before the person bearing the name attained the age of eighteen years or [illegible]

§ Directorships.—The names of all bodies corporate incorporated in Great Britain of which the director is also a director should be given, except bodies corporate of which the company making the return is the wholly-owned subsidiary or bodies corporate which are the wholly-owned subsidiaries either of the Company or of another Company of which the Company is the wholly-owned subsidiary. A body corporate is deemed to be the wholly-owned subsidiary of another if it has no members except that other and that other's wholly-owned subsidiaries and its or their nominees.

‖ Dates of birth need only be given in the case of a company which is subject to section 185 of the Companies Act, 1948, namely, a company which is not a private company or which, being a private company, is the subsidiary of a body corporate incorporated in the United Kingdom which is neither a private company nor a company registered under the law relating to companies for the time being in force in Northern

REGISTER OF DIRECTORS' SHARE & DEBENTURE INTERESTS

Director's Name..

PARTICULARS OF RIGHTS GRANTED TO DIRECTORS TO SUBSCRIBE FOR THE COMPANY'S SHARES OR DEBENTURES (see Note 2 below)											NOTIFICATION BY DIRECTOR OF INTERESTS IN SHARES OR DEBENTURES, OR CESSATION, SALE OR ASSIGNMENT OF SUCH INTERESTS (see Notes 2 (ii) and 3 below)						Date of Entry	Remarks
RIGHTS GRANTED								RIGHTS TAKEN UP			Date of Interest or Sale or Assignment of Interest	Particulars of Interest or of Sale or Assignment of Interest	Shares or Debentures Involved			Date of notification		
Date Right Granted	Operative Period of Right		Consideration (state if "none")	Shares or Debs Involved			Date Taken up	Shares or Debentures Taken Up					Issuing Company	Class	Number or Amount			
	From	To		Class	Number or Amount	Price to be Paid		Class	Number or Amount	Person(s) in whose Name(s) Registered								

Director's Name..

Date Right Granted	From	To	Consideration	Class	Number or Amount	Price to be Paid	Date Taken up	Class	Number or Amount	Person(s) in whose Name(s) Registered	Date of Interest or Sale or Assignment of Interest	Particulars of Interest or of Sale or Assignment of Interest	Issuing Company	Class	Number or Amount	Date of notification	Date of Entry	Remarks

NOTES

The main provisions governing registration of a Director's Share and Debenture Interests are contained in Schedules 27 to 31 of the Companies Act, 1967, and may be summarised as follows:

1. Names of Directors must appear in alphabetical order, otherwise an index must be kept. Entries in the Register must be in chronological order.
2. (i) The Company must, within 3 days, register details:
   (a) of any right given to a Director to subscribe for the Company's Shares or Debentures;
   (b) of the exercise of any such right.
   (ii) Where any such right is assigned to or exercised by a Director's spouse or infant child the Director must notify the Company, in writing, within 14 days; and the Company must enter the particulars in the Register within 3 days from receipt of the notification.
3. A Director must notify the Company of any Interest in Shares or Debentures of the Company, or of the Company's subsidiary or holding company, or in any subsidiary of the holding company, or of the cessation, sale or assignment of any such interest. An interest under a trust owning such Shares or Debentures (other than a discretionary interest) should be similarly notified.
   Such notifications must be made by the Director in writing within 14 days following the event, and the company must enter the particulars in the Register within 3 days from receipt of the notification.
4. Saturdays, Sundays and Bank Holidays are ignored in reckoning the time limits, for notification and registration, stated above.
5. A person in accordance with whose directions the Directors of a company are accustomed to act is deemed to be a Director for the purpose of these provisions.
6. A person shall be deemed to have an Interest in the Company's Shares or Debentures if a body corporate is interested in them and:
   (a) the directors of that body corporate are accustomed to act in accordance with his directions, or;
   (b) he controls one-third or more of the voting power of that body corporate.
7. The register shall be kept at the office at which the Company's register of members is kept, and shall be open for inspections by members or any other persons for not less than two hours a day during normal business hours. The Register must be produced and made available for inspection at the Company's annual general meeting.

5. LIST OF PAST AND PRESENT MEMBERS.

Members holding shares or stock in the company on the fourteenth day after the annual general meeting for 19........, and of persons who have held shares or stock therein at any time since the date of the last return, or in the case of the first return, of the incorporation of the company.§||

Names and Addresses (N.B.—Christian or forenames of past and present members should be shown in full as well as surnames.)	Number of shares held by existing members at date of return*†	Account of Shares			REMARKS
		‡Particulars of Shares Transferred since the date of the last Return, or (in the case of the first Return) of the incorporation of the Company, by (a) persons who are still Members, and, (b) persons who have ceased to be Members.			
		Number†	Date of registration of transfer		
			(a)	(b)	

§ If the names in this return are not arranged in alphabetical order, an index sufficient to enable the name of any person in the list to be readily found must be annexed to this List.

|| If the return for either of the two immediately preceding years has given as at the date of that return the full particulars required as to past and present members and the shares and stock held and transferred by them, only such of the particulars need be given as relate to persons ceasing to be or becoming members since the date of the last return and to shares transferred since that date or to changes as compared with that date in the amount of stock held by a member.

* The aggregate number of shares held by each member must be stated, and the aggregates must be added up so as to agree with the number of shares stated in the Summary of Share Capital and Debentures to have been taken up.

† When the shares are of different classes these columns should be sub-divided so that the number of each class held, or transferred, may be shown separately. Where any shares have been converted into stock the amount of stock held by each member must be shown.

‡ The date of registration of each transfer should be given as well as the number of shares transferred on each date. The particulars should be placed opposite the name of the transferor and not opposite that of the

6. PARTICULARS OF DIRECTORS* AND SECRETARIES.

Particulars of the persons who are directors of the company at the date of this return.

PRESENT CHRISTIAN NAME OR NAMES AND SURNAME (in the case of a corporation the corporate name)**	Any former Christian Name or Names and Surname‡	Nationality	USUAL RESIDENTIAL ADDRESS (in the case of a corporation, the registered or principal office)	Business Occupation and particulars of other Directorships§	Date of Birth‖

Particulars of the person who is secretary of the company at the date of this return.

†THE PRESENT CHRISTIAN NAME OR NAMES AND SURNAME	Any former Christian Name or Names and Surname‡	USUAL RESIDENTIAL ADDRESS.

NOTES

* "Director" includes any person who occupies the position of a Director by whatsoever name called, and any person in accordance with whose directions or instructions the directors of the company are accustomed to act.

† "Christian name" includes a forename, and "surname," in the case of a peer or person usually known by a title different from his Surname, means that title.

‡ "Former Christian name" and "former surname" do not include—

(*a*) In the case of a peer or a person usually known by a British title different from his surname, the name by which he was known previous to the adoption of or succession to the title; or

(*b*) In the case of any person, a former Christian name or surname where that name or surname was changed or disused before the person bearing the name attained the age of eighteen years or has been changed or disused for a period of not less than twenty years; or

(*c*) In the case of a married woman the name or surname by which she was known previous to the marriage.

§ Directorships.—The names of all bodies corporate incorporated in Great Britain of which the director is also a director should be given, except bodies corporate of which the company making the return is the wholly-owned subsidiary or bodies corporate which are the wholly-owned subsidiaries either of the company or of another company of which the company is the wholly-owned subsidiary. A body corporate is deemed to be the wholly-owned subsidiary of another if it has no members except that other and that other's wholly-owned subsidiaries and its or their nominees. If the space provided in the form is insufficient, particulars of other directorships should be listed on a separate statement attached to this form.

‖ Dates of birth need only be given in the case of a company which is subject to section 185 of the Companies Act, 1948, namely, a company which is not a private company or which, being a private company, is the subsidiary of a body corporate incorporated in the United Kingdom which is neither a private company nor a company registered under the law relating to companies for the time being in force in Northern Ireland and having provisions in its constitution which would, if it had been registered in Great Britain, entitle it to rank as a private company.

** Where all the partners in a firm are joint secretaries, the name and principal office of the firm may be stated.

MINUTES

.... Dated.............................19........... Folio in Register........................

No..................... ....**Shares**

....

LIMITED

Incorporated under the Companies Act, 19

CAPITAL - - - - - £

Divided into

This is to Certify that.. of..

is the Registered Proprietor of.. Shares of £ each, in the above-named Company, numbered from to inclusive, subject to the Memorandum and Articles of Association of the Company, and that upon each of such Shares the sum of £ has been paid.

Given under the Common Seal of the above Company, this.............................. day of.............................. 19..........

.... }
.... } Directors

.... Secretary

NOTE.—No transfer of any of the above-mentioned Shares can be registered until this Certificate has been deposited at the Company's Registered Office.

4.6 The Ongoing Running of Your Corporation

There are certain rules and regulations that you must comply with after you have formed your corporation (see Appendix A). In the main they apply to your accounts. (Keep a strict record of all your transactions whether it be a petty cash receipt or the purchase of business premises.) There are a number of individual accounting companies who specialise in keeping books for the small businessman. Their services can be of tremendous value to you. Their charges are usually reasonable and they look after your normal accounts and your VAT and can usually produce an up-to-date balance of your accounts on request (always needed for your bank manager when you need that loan fast). When your accounting year comes up, they will have made the accountant's job a simple one. At the same time they will help to keep your auditor's costs down to a reasonable level.

4.7 Final Checklist

We now come to the final checklist. If you tick each item as you complete it you will have an up-to-date record on the formation of your company.

		Tick when completed
(1)	Send off to Companies Registration Office for Forms No PUC1, No 10 and No 12	[ ]
(2)	Get a 'good' name	[ ]
(3)	Check availability of selected title	[ ]
(4)	Draft Memorandum & Articles of Association	[ ]
(5)	Fill in Forms No PUC1, No 10, No 12	[ ]
(6)	Commissioner of Oaths to attest Form No 12	[ ]
(7)	Send to Companies House:	
	• completed Forms No PUC1, No 10, No 12	[ ]
	• registration fee £50	[ ]
	• Memorandum & Articles of Association	[ ]
(8)	On arrival of Certificate of Incorporation:	
	• order company seal/company sign	[ ]
	• create or purchase the company register	[ ]
	• order business stationery	[ ]
	• make further sets of Mem & Arts	[ ]
	• open bank account	[ ]
	• decide whether you will need to be registered for VAT	[ ]
	• hold first meeting of directors	[ ]
	• issue shares	[ ]
	• send off Form No PUC2	[ ]
	• enter all relevant details in company register	[ ]
(9)	Commence business	[ ]
(10)	Within six months complete and return Form No 224 (Notice of accounts reference date) to the CRO	[ ]

5

Company Formation in Offshore Areas

I have included this chapter on offshore companies to give you an insight into the different areas and their tax position. Most people who become involved in offshore formations do so to alleviate their tax burden in the countries in which they reside. They also do it for confidentiality. There are several areas throughout the world where it is especially tax advantageous to locate a company. The formation of companies is different for each area, so I have only partly covered the areas concerned.

The first part of this chapter deals with Britain's offshore islands. The second part deals with overseas company formations. The third part covers the types of offshore companies and the use that can be made of them.

5.1 Britain's Offshore Islands

Isle of Man

The Isle of Man is not part of the United Kingdom but is rather a self-governing territory within the Commonwealth. It is, of course, an independent taxation area. The Isle of Man is associated with the EEC and has an income tax rate of 20 per cent levied on individuals and companies alike. There is generally no need to disclose details of beneficial ownership of companies to the insular authorities so that, with the abolition of Sterling Area exchange controls by the Bank of England, companies can be formed quite discreetly. Generally the Isle of Man has no stamp duty on transfer of property, no capital transfer tax, no surtax, no corporation tax, no wealth tax, no death duties and no gift tax. There is no capital gains tax except in respect of certain land transactions in the Island itself. Value added tax is collected by the Isle of Man Customs and Excise at the same rate as applies in the United Kingdom.

One of the main advantages of the Isle of Man from an investor's point of view, however, is its great political stability; it enjoys parliamentary government without party politics. Indeed, in 1979, Tynwald – the Island parliament – celebrated its millennium. The Island has thus enjoyed a steady and well-regulated growth in its financial sector. Because it has other industries, the Isle of Man is now established as an important international financial centre that is at once reputable and has a 'low profile'.

Resident companies pay Isle of Man income tax at

20 per cent after allowances have been computed. Companies are regarded as being resident in the Isle of Man if the majority of directors are resident in the Isle of Man and meet in the Isle of Man. Non-resident companies pay no tax on the income that they receive outside the Island but rather pay a fixed Company Registration Tax of £250 per annum, irrespective of the magnitude of their profits. Companies are regarded as being resident outside the Isle of Man if the majority of directors reside and meet outside the Isle of Man.

The concept of the residence of a company being where its central management and control are exercised and, therefore, where its directors meet is essential to most Isle of Man tax advantage companies. There are firms that provide directors for Isle of Man companies so that a company may be regarded as being either resident or non-resident. In this regard it should be borne in mind that many countries use residence as the test for taxation of companies, so that such firms would stress their ability to provide directors from countries that would not lead to an Isle of Man company becoming embroiled within another taxation area.

An Isle of Man company must also have its registered office within the Isle of Man and it is an administrative requirement that there should be a Manx resident company secretary or director to carry out the maintenance of statutory books, filing and dealings with the Isle of Man authorities. There are specialist companies that provide these domiciliation services together with mailing, telephone, telex and cable answering services.

The Channel Islands of Guernsey and Jersey

The Channel Islands of Guernsey and Jersey are both independent tax areas, being internally autonomous possessions of the British Crown. Both Islands are well-established financial centres; their growth in both facilities and expertise was greatly encouraged by British investors using the Islands in years of exchange control restriction. The Islands benefit from their proximity to both Europe and Britain for, whilst the free trade aspects of the EEC apply, tax harmonisation policies do not.

Guernsey and Jersey each have their own legislatures and tax laws, but in both cases a company that has its central management and control exercised locally (that is, where its board of directors would meet in the Island of its incorporation) pays tax at a rate of 20 per cent on its worldwide income. Alternatively, a company may be externally controlled with its directors meeting outside the Island of incorporation. Such a company would be called a corporation tax company paying a registration tax of £3,000 yearly in advance. Generally there is no capital gains tax, no estate duty and no tax on wealth or goods. It is of interest to note, too, that no value added tax is collected on the Islands.

Company formation in Guernsey and Jersey, although by process of the Royal Court, is a relatively straightforward procedure, with formation times being about one or two weeks. The Law Officers of the Crown in Guernsey and the Commercial Relations Department in Jersey vet applications to form new companies in line with the 1927 Accord between the Islands and the UK government for the purpose of preventing the avoidance of taxation by UK residents.

Again, there are specialist companies that provide nominee incorporators as well as continuing management services to Channel Islands companies, including provision of registered offices and the making of annual returns.

Gibraltar

Gibraltar is a financial centre that enjoys increasing popularity. Gibraltar companies would normally pay tax at a rate of 37.5 per cent, but, under the Companies (Taxation and Concessions) Ordinance, 1967, exempt status may be granted by virtue of which no local tax is paid. An exempt status company may carry on its business in any part of the world provided that no Gibraltarian residents are interested in, or trade with, the company. Exempt status is granted at the discretion of the government's Financial and Development Secretary. Upon approval of the application, a certificate is granted that remains in effect for 25 years, provided that the company is otherwise maintained in good standing. Where the beneficial owners are residents of the United Kingdom, the exempt company must not trade with the United Kingdom.

Exempt companies may be managed within Gibraltar and classified as ordinarily resident, paying an annual fee of £225. Should a company be managed from outside Gibraltar, it pays a fee of £200 per annum. The advantage of an ordinarily resident exempt company is that it may be presumed not to be resident elsewhere. Once again, there are companies whose services include the provision of directors to achieve these designations as well as full domiciliation service. Gibraltar companies can be incorporated in 10–14 days. However, the exempt status application can take four or more weeks to process.

The United Kingdom

The principle of a company's liability for tax being based on its residence is one that was developed more than 70 years ago in the UK. By virtue of this principle, United Kingdom 'tax haven' companies may be set up. These companies are owned and managed by non-residents of the United Kingdom and, in order to be treated as tax exempt structures by the Inland Revenue, they would normally avoid trading with or investing in the United Kingdom. If a company incorporated in the United Kingdom is from the beginning managed and controlled abroad, there is no need to apply to the Inland Revenue to be designated non-resident, although certain enquiries will have to be answered to put the Inland Revenue in possession of the facts. Non-resident companies would be exempt from the flat-rate annual registration taxes that now apply in so many tax havens. One clear advantage of their use is that United Kingdom company structures are generally respected and are not readily identified as tax haven entities.

The major disadvantage of using UK companies is that shareholding and, in particular, details of accounts have to be filed annually so that a foreign fiscal authority may be able to make accurate deductions from the public records. In all parts of the United Kingdom stamp duty is levied on share subscriptions and transfers and the shares of a UK company are regarded as UK assets for capital transfer considerations.

Northern Ireland and Scotland

The Department of Trade maintains two Registries for companies incorporated in Great Britain: at Cardiff for those having their registered office in England and Wales, and at Edinburgh for those with a registered office in Scotland. Northern Ireland operates separate Companies Acts and its Registry is maintained in Belfast.

Exchange control

The British Islands no longer have an exchange control system. Previously, the Scheduled Territories of the Sterling Area consisted of the United Kingdom, the Channel Islands, the Isle of Man, the Republic of Ireland, and Gibraltar, and controls were applied by the Bank of England in respect of transactions with non-residents of the Sterling Area. Now British residents and British companies may freely invest abroad, and similarly non-residents may freely invest in Britain or her offshore areas.

5.2 Overseas Company Formations

Anguilla

The island of Anguilla is located in the East Caribbean. It was part of St Kitts – officially St Christopher, Nevis and Anguilla – until 1967, when it effectively became a separate British colony.

In the Anguilla Act 1971 – an Act of the Westminster Parliament – provision was made for the future administration of the Island and, since February 1976, Anguilla has had its own constitution, which for practical purposes gives Anguilla the status of a British Dependent Territory.

In 1977 the legislature formally suspended the St Kitts Income Tax Act. Anguilla has specifically chosen to have no income tax, companies tax or death duties and it is believed that this will make the Island more attractive for outside investors. Anguilla has no exchange control regulations and there is therefore no restriction on the mobility of funds. Its currency is the East Caribbean dollar, which is tied to the United States dollar.

The Companies Law of Anguilla is based upon earlier United Kingdom legislation. Anguilla can be used as a corporate domicile for trading, investment, shipping and property companies. An Anguillan company can trade in any part of the world and, if necessary, register branch offices in foreign countries. Anguilla permits bearer shares.

Anguilla has strict control of banking so far as companies operating in Anguilla are concerned, this activity being governed by the Banking Act 1967, as amended. However, for companies operating offshore, application may be made for a 'B' banking licence ('A' banking licences being for banks dealing with the Anguillan public). An offshore bank would have to show a capital of US $187,000 and each year pay an annual licence fee of US $7506.

The Insurance Act makes no specific provision for offshore operation but it is possible to be exempted from its otherwise restrictive requirements. Anguilla is a British port of registry under Merchant Shipping Acts and is a convenient base for the registration of ships and pleasure craft.

Delaware – gateway to the United States

Delaware is a small US state that is marked by few regulations and a lack of bureaucracy in arranging its affairs. Corporation service companies throughout the United States consider the Delaware corporation law among the most attractive for organisation purposes and the state of Delaware a valuable jurisdiction in which to organise new companies.

The outstanding advantages of incorporating in Delaware are as follows: corporations not having any business in Delaware pay no Delaware corporate income tax; the fees payable to the state of Delaware are based upon the number of shares of authorised capital stock, with the no par shares fee one-half of the par shares fee; the franchise tax compares favourably with that for any other state; shares of stock owned by persons outside the state are not subject to taxation; shares of stock that are part of the estate of a non-resident decedent are exempt from the state Inheritance Tax Law.

The policy of Delaware courts has always been to construe the corporation law liberally, to interpret any ambiguities or uncertainties in the working of the statutes so as to reach a reasonable and fair construction. The careful investor can therefore have confidence in the security of the investment.

Whilst some states insist that one director, at least, should be a US citizen, there is no restriction in Delaware on the nationality of directors of corporations set up in the state. It should be noted, however, that Delaware corporations do fall within the federal tax system.

Panama

The Republic of Panama is located in Central America and lies between Costa Rica and Columbia. It has excellent transport and communication. Panama is a long-established tax haven and is known for its shipping registration. The financial sector of its economy provides the best facilities in Latin America, with all the principal banks of the world being represented. There is complete freedom in the movement of funds. All business is conducted in United States dollars and there are no exchange control problems.

Although Panama has fairly high rates of tax internally, its status as a tax haven depends upon the principle that income received by a Panamanian corporation from sources outside Panama is exempt from tax. The activities not subject to tax are:

(a) invoicing, from an office established in Panama,

the sale of merchandise or products for a sum higher than that at which said products or merchandise had been invoiced to the office established in Panama, provided that said merchandise or products are handled exclusively abroad;

(b) directing, from an office in Panama, operations that are completed, consummated or take effect abroad; and

(c) distributing dividends or participations from income not produced when said dividends or participations are derived from income not produced within the territory of the Republic of Panama, including the income derived from activities mentioned in subdivisions (a) and (b) of this proviso.

The Panamanian company law is an adaptation of the law of Delaware as it was stated in 1927 and for reasons of constancy little amendment has been made. It is characterised by its flexibility: directors (a minimum of three) and officers can be non-resident and directors' and shareholders' meetings can take place anywhere in the world. Panama also permits bearer shares. Incorporation time is in the order of two weeks and company names can use any of the following designations: Sociedad Anonima, Corporation or Incorporated (or S.A. Corp. or Inc.).

Liberia

Liberia is situated on the West Coast of Africa. It is mainly known for its shipping registration facilities, but corporations organised in Liberia may be useful for any type of trading operation or investment activity that would be satisfied by the territorial principle of income tax, which would generally exempt all foreign source income. Although income tax is levied on local operations, no taxes are imposed on Liberian corporations provided that (a) more than 50 per cent of the corporation's stock is held by non-Liberians and (b) all corporate income is derived from sources outside Liberia.

Liberia has modelled its company law on that for the state of Delaware, and the Business Corporation Act of 1976 is the latest consolidation of liberal interpretation by the courts of the earlier Delaware law. Directors, officers or stockholders of a Liberian company may reside anywhere in the world. The company's head office may again be located anywhere, so that the company need have little dealing with its place of incorporation. Shares may be held in either registered or bearer form. The bearer form – together with the fact that changes in shareholders and directors need not be recorded after incorporation – gives the beneficial owner almost complete anonymity. This is furthered by the fact that the Liberian representative of the company is not required to file reports to the government on the activities of the company.

Incorporation itself, which must be carried out by members of the legal profession, can be a rapid procedure. Liberia uses English as the official language employing English letters and characters that show the fact that the name is the name of a company.

Please note

The 'specialist companies' to which I refer can be found in the business columns of the main Sunday newspapers (in particular the *Sunday Times*).

5.3 Examples of Offshore Companies

The following examples illustrate the use that can be made of offshore companies. However, the tax and other benefits that can be obtained by use of an offshore company will depend on the country of residence of the beneficial owner and its anti-avoidance legislation.

Investment companies
Funds accumulated through investment companies set up in many offshore areas can be invested or deposited throughout the world. While they will be subject to the tax regimes of the countries of investment, there are many tax-free bonds or bank deposits where interest is paid gross. Capital gains tax is not paid in some jurisdictions by overseas companies.

Trading companies
These companies may act as distributors or sale companies. The offshore company will take orders directly from the customer but have the goods delivered directly to him from the manufacturer or place of purchase. The profits arising on the difference between purchase price and sales price may then be accumulated either free of tax or at a low tax rate.

Professional services companies
Individuals who receive substantial fees in respect of

their professonal services, such as designers, consultants, authors or entertainers, may assign or contract with an offshore company the right to receive those fees. The offshore company may then accumulate that income in a low tax or no-tax environment with such accumulations perhaps being invested to generate further income for the offshore company.

Shipping companies

Shipping companies can eliminate direct or indirect taxation on ships registered under the flags of international shipping havens like Panama, Liberia or Anguilla. They may also own or charter ships, profits from which can be accumulated tax free. With regard to the registration of ships or yachts at British ports of registry such as Anguilla, the Isle of Man, the Channel Islands or Gibraltar, the ship can be surveyed at a number of ports throughout the world provided that the surveyor is recognised by the UK Department of Trade and Industry. The British flag has always been regarded as one of the world's most dependable.

Royalty companies

An offshore company can purchase or be assigned the right to use a copyright, patent, trademark or know-how with a power to sub-license. It can then accumulate royalties in the tax haven area, although often royalties may suffer withholding taxes at source. In some cases an interposing holding company may allow a reduction in the rate of tax withheld at source.

Banking companies

Many offshore banking institutions have been established in tax havens in recent years. Many of these institutions are subsidiaries of major international banks. Such institutions may pay interest free of withholding taxes and engage in international financing from tax haven bases in which no effective exchange control restrictions are applied. Established banking havens such as the Bahamas and the Cayman Islands restrict the setting up of new institutions through capitalisation and licensing requirements generally. Developing havens such as Anguilla, on the other hand, are keen to encourage the setting up of smaller banking companies to stimulate local investment and job creation.

Insurance companies

Some havens are keen to encourage the setting up of insurance companies, which, like banking companies, bring employment and investment to the country of incorporation and generally enhance its range of financial services. Captive insurance companies have been created by many multinational companies to insure and reinsure the risks of groups of affiliated companies. Bermuda has long been favoured as a site for the incorporation of captives, with countries such as the Turks and Caicos Islands, Anguilla and the Isle of Man competing for a share of this growing market.

6

Companies Registered Overseas

This chapter is intended to serve as a guide to the essential requirements for overseas companies under the Companies Act 1985, to which reference should be made at all times.

All enquiries relating to overseas companies in England and Wales should be addressed to the Registrar of Companies, Companies House, Crown Ways, Maindy, Cardiff CF4 3UZ.

6.1 Requirement to Register

Within one month of establishing a place of business in Great Britain, overseas companies are required to deliver to the Registrar of Companies the following documents and forms for registration under Section 691 of the Companies Act 1985:

- A certified copy of the charter, statutes of Memorandum and Articles of the company, or other instruments constituting or defining the constitution of the company, and, if the instrument is not written in the English language, a certified translation. These documents or instruments must be listed on Form 691.

- A list and particulars of the directors and secretary of the company on Form 691.
- Form 691 giving the names and addresses of one or more persons resident in Great Britain authorised to accept on behalf of the company any notices required to be served on the company.
- Declaration by an overseas company of the establishment of a place of business in Great Britain on Form 691.

6.2 Names

Control over the names used in Great Britain by overseas companies is exercised under Section 694 of the 1985 Act. The effect is to apply the same criteria to the names of overseas companies and British companies (see Chapter 2 above). Briefly, a company is not allowed to register by a name that is the same as that of any other organisation on the Index of Company Names maintained by the Registrar, or that is considered offensive, or whose use would constitute a criminal offence. The Secretary of State also has power to refuse a proposed name where:

- the name as a whole might give the impression that the company was connected with HM Government or a local authority, or

- the name contains certain words or expressions specified in the regulations.

Following the registration of documents, if the name submitted is not acceptable a Notice may be served on the company within 12 months of the date on which the company has complied with the requirements of the Acts in respect of delivery of documents as in section 6.1 above, or section 6.3 below. The Notice will give reasons for the non-acceptability of the name. Where a Notice has been served on the company to change its name, a Form 694(a) giving details of the new name under which the company proposes to carry on business in Great Britain must be delivered to the Registrar. If the proposed name is still not acceptable, a new name should be submitted on Form 694(b).

An overseas company registered in Great Britain that proposes to operate a business with a name other than its corporate name should refer to the *Notes for Guidance on Business Names and Disclosure of Business Ownership* for further details (available from Companies House).

6.3 Alteration of Particulars Already Registered

If any alteration is made after registration to any of the particulars delivered to the Registrar of Companies, the company must notify the Registrar of the alteration by delivering:

- amended and certified charter and statutes and,

where necessary, certified translations (under cover of Form 692(1)a);

- notification of any change of name (under cover of Form 692(2)) accompanied by a change of name certificate or a copy of the relevant resolution;
- an amended list of the directors and secretary of the company (on Form 692(1)b);
- the names and addresses of one or more persons resident in Great Britain authorised to accept on behalf of the company service of process and any notices required to be served (on Form 692(1)c).

6.4 Accounts

An overseas company is required to prepare and deliver accounts and to determine the accounting reference period as laid down in Sections 700–701 of the Companies Act 1985. Notice of the accounting reference date must be forwarded on Form 701(2) within six months of registration in Great Britain. A company may change its accounting reference date in certain circumstances. This change must be notified to the Registrar on Form 701(6)a if the change is during the course of an accounting reference period, or on Form 701(6)b if the change is after the end of an accounting reference period, and is to coincide with the accounting reference date for a holding or subsidiary company.

Accounts should be delivered within 13 months of the end of the accounting reference period. Reference should be made to the Act for special provisions – for example, those dealing with the time allowed to overseas companies newly established in Great Britain.

Each year a balance sheet and profit and loss account of the company in the country of incorporation must be filed with the Registrar of Companies. An auditor's report is not required. Group accounts should be included if the parent company is a holding company. Certified translations should also be filed where a foreign language is used. A registration fee of £20 is payable.

6.5 Registration of Charges (Including Mortgages) (Sections 409–424 of the Companies Act 1985)

An overseas company that has an established place of business in England, Wales or Scotland, is required to send particulars of certain charges created to the Registrar for registration. The forms to be used are:

- Form 395/410(Scot) (if in Scotland) – particulars of a mortgage or charge on property in England
- Form 400/416(Scot) – particulars of mortgage or charge on property in England or Wales that has been acquired
- Form 397/413(Scot) – particulars of a series of debentures

- Form 397a/413a(Scot) – particulars of an issue of debentures in a series
- Form 403a/419a(Scot) – declaration and memorandum of complete satisfaction
- Form 403a/419a(Scot) – declaration and memorandum of partial satisfaction or release of part of property.
- Form 403b/419b(Scot) – declaration and memorandum that part of the property mortgaged or charged has ceased to form part of the company's property
- Form 403b/466(Scot) – particulars of an alteration to a floating charge.

6.6 Obligation to Exhibit Certain Information

The company must exhibit conspicuously on every place where it establishes a place of business, and on all billheads and letter paper, the names of the company, the country in which the company is incorporated and whether the liability of its members is limited (Sections 348–351 of the Companies Act 1985). If the company chooses to give details of any director on letterheads or stationery, it must give the same details of all the directors.

6.7 Channel Islands and Isle of Man Companies

An annual return of Form 363 must also be delivered to the Registrar.

Appendix A

Guide to Statutory Requirements

The following appendix is intended to serve as a guide to some of the requirements of the 1985 Companies Act but, as much of it is set out in an abbreviated form, reference should be made at all times to the relevant provisions of the Act and statutory instruments for fuller information.

Accounting Requirements

(1) Accounts

Every company must keep accounting records, comprehensive enough to disclose with reasonable accuracy, at any time, the financial position of the company at that time. Records must be kept of the daily receipt and disbursement of money, the assets, liabilities, stocktaking records at the end of the financial year, and, except for retail sales, sufficient detail to enable the goods and the buyers and sellers to be identified. Such accounting records shall be kept, in the case of a private company, for three years and in any other case for six years (Section 222(4) of the 1985 Act). From its accounting records the company's accounts must be prepared at certain specific periods, comprising:

- a profit and loss account, or income and expenditure account if appropriate;

- a balance sheet as at the date of the profit and loss account;
- an auditor's report;
- a directors' report (see also para. 18 below); and, if appropriate,
- group accounts.

(2) Accounting reference date

Every company may if it wishes notify the Registrar (on Form No 224) of the date on which its accounting reference period will end in each year. This is known as the company's accounting reference date. If it does not notify a particular accounting reference date to the Registrar within six months of its incorporation he will regard the company's accounting reference date as being 31 March (Section 224(3) of the 1985 Act).

Each year the company must produce its accounts made up to the accounting reference date. The financial year is the period covered by the accounts (Section 227 of the 1985 Act).

(3) New companies and their first accounting reference period

A new company's first accounting reference period begins on its incorporation and runs until the accounting reference date as notified to (or imposed by) the Registrar is first reached – except that, if this would result in the period being less than six months in duration, it will run to the second occasion on which the accounting reference date is reached. The first accounting reference period may not exceed 18 months (Section 224(4) of the 1985 Act).

(4) Changing the accounting reference date
Provisions are made to allow a company to change the accounting reference date notified to the Registrar in certain circumstances, on Form No 225(1) or 225(2).

(i) Form No 225(1) is to be used to extend or shorten the current accounting reference period and notice is to be given before the expiry of its current accounting reference period.

NB The accounting reference date cannot be extended more than once in five years unless the company is aligning its accounting reference date with that of a holding or subsidiary company.

(ii) Form No 225(2) is for use by a company aligning its accounting reference date with that of its holding or subsidiary company after the end of the accounting reference period. The notice must be given before the expiration of the period allowed for laying and delivering accounts relating to the old accounting reference period (Section 225 (2) of the 1985 Act).

(5) Duty to deliver a copy of the accounts
(i) A company, irrespective of whether or not it is trading, is required to:

(a) lay before the company's members in general meeting the accounts prepared in respect of each accounting reference period;
(b) deliver a copy of the accounts to the Registrar of Companies unless throughout the accounting reference period the following conditions were satisfied:

- the company is unlimited, and it is not a subsidiary of, or the holding company for, a limited company, and
- it has not carried out business as a trading stamp scheme promoter.

(ii) Every balance sheet of a company and every copy that is laid before the company in general meeting or delivered to the Registrar under Section 238 of the 1985 Act shall be signed on behalf of the board by two of the directors of the company or, if there is only one director, by that director (Section 238(1),(2)).

Copies of balance sheets other than those laid before the company or delivered to the Registrar which are issued, circulated or published by a company may bear copy signatures. Such copy signatures, whether manuscript, typescript or printed, should reproduce the exact style of the original signature (e.g. if the 'live' signature on the balance sheet were 'John Ernest Brown', it would not be sufficient to print 'J. E. Brown' on the copy circulated to shareholders.

The balance sheet of a banking company registered after 15 August 1979 must be signed by the secretary or manager, if any, and, where there are more than three directors of the company, by at least three of those directors, and, where there are not more than three directors, by all the directors (Section 238 of the 1985 Act).

(iii) The accounts must be laid before the company and delivered to the Registrar within time limits, which vary between private companies and public companies.

(a) *Private companies*

The accounts must be laid before the company and delivered to the Registrar within ten months of the end of the accounting reference period.

(b) *Public companies*
The accounts must be laid before the company and delivered to the Registrar within seven months of the end of the accounting reference period.

(c) *Companies with overseas interests*
If in any particular accounting reference period a company, whether private or public, carried on business or has interests outside the United Kingdom, the Channel Isles and the Isle of Man, the company may serve notice on the Registrar (Form No 242) stating that the company has such overseas business and/or interests and claim an extension of three months in the time allowed for the laying and delivering of accounts.

(d) *New companies*
Where a newly incorporated company has as its first accounting reference period a period in excess of 12 months as described in paragraph 3 above, the period allowed for laying and delivering accounts will be reduced by the amount of time by which the accounting reference period exceeded 12 months. However, the period allowed for delivery of accounts will not be reduced to less than three months.

(iv) The accounting exemptions in Sections 247–253 of the 1985 Act permit certain companies to deliver modified accounts to the Registrar of Companies for filing.

Two classes of companies will be able to take advantage of these concessions:

(a) *Small companies* that satisfy at least two of the following criteria:

- turnover not exceeding £1,400,000
- balance sheet total not exceeding £700,000
- average number of employees not exceeding 50

may submit only an abbreviated balance sheet and a limited number of notes thereon.

(b) *Medium-sized companies* that satisfy two of the following criteria:

- turnover not exceeding £5,750,000
- balance sheet total not exceeding £2,800,000
- average number of employees not exceeding 250

must submit a profit and loss account, a balance sheet and a directors' report. However, the profit and loss account may be abbreviated and need not disclose turnover.

To claim the accounting exemptions, a set of accounts delivered to the Registrar must include:

(i) a statement by the directors, immediately above their signatures on the balance sheet, that they have relied on the exemptions for individual accounts and that they have done so on the ground that the company is entitled to the benefit of those exemptions as a small company or a medium-sized company as the case may be;

(ii) a special auditor's report, stating that in the opinion of the auditors the requirements for exemption are satisfied and reproducing in full the auditor's report made under Section 236 of the 1985 Act on the full accounts prepared under Section 221 of the Act.

(v) Ineligible companies
The exemptions described above are not available to public companies, banking, insurance or shipping companies regardless of size.

(vi) All companies must still prepare full accounts for the benefit of the members of the company.

(vii) The accounting exemptions are not mandatory and small and medium-sized companies may continue to deliver full sets of accounts to the Registrar if they wish to do so.

(viii) Dormant companies
A company that is entitled to claim the accounting exemptions for small companies and that is for the time being dormant may pass a special resolution at a general meeting at which accounts are laid (or before its first such meeting if it is a newly formed company) to exclude Section 384 of the Companies Act 1985 from applying to the company, which thus becomes exempt from the obligation to appoint an auditor.

A company is regarded as being dormant during any period in which no transaction occurs that is a significant accounting transaction required to be entered in the company's accounting records under Section 221 of the Companies Act 1985.

A company that is dormant and that has passed a special resolution as described above may deliver to the Registrar accounts consisting of a balance sheet containing above the signature of the directors a statement that the company was dormant, within the meaning of Section 252 of the Companies Act 1985, throughout the financial year ending with the date of the balance sheet.

If a company ceases to be dormant or ceases in any other way to qualify to exclude the obligation to appoint auditors, it ceases to be so exempt and the directors may appoint an auditor to serve until the end of the next general meeting of the company. Alternatively, if the directors fail to exercise this power, the company in general meeting may appoint an auditor.

(6) Overseas companies

The accounting requirements described above, with the exception of the UK auditor's report (Statutory Instrument No 1786 of 1980 – The Overseas Companies (Accounts) (Exceptions) Order 1980), also apply to overseas companies registered in the United Kingdom under Part XXIII of the 1985 Act. There are other variations, which are set out in Sections 700–701 of the 1985 Act.

Shares and Capital

(7) Maintenance of capital

Where the net assets of a public company are reduced to half or less of the amount of the company's called-up share capital, the directors of the company shall within 28 days of that fact becoming known to them convene an extraordinary general meeting to be held within 56 days from that date, to consider what measures, if any, should be taken to deal with the situation (Section 142 of the 1985 Act).

(8) Distribution of profits and assets

A company shall not make a distribution except out of realised profits less its accumulated realised losses, or, in the case of a public company, if such distribution would reduce its net assets below the sum of its called-up share capital and undistributable reserves (Sections 263 and 264 of the 1985 Act).

(9) Allotments

If a limited company having a share capital makes an allowance of shares for cash, it must file a return of allotment with the Registrar within one month on Form No PUC2. If shares are allotted for a consideration other than cash the return must be made on Form No PUC3 and the company must also file a contract in writing constituting the title of the allottee to the allotment, together with any contract of sales or, in the case of a private company, a contract for services relative to the making of the allotment. Where the contract is not in writing the prescribed particulars of the contract stamped with the same stamp duty as on a contract should be given on Form No 88(3) (Section 88 of the 1985 Act). Where a claim for credit or relief from capital duty is made under Section 5(5) of the Finance Act 1973, a Form No PUC4 should accompany the appropriate PUC form.

Forms Nos PUC2 and PUC3 bear Inland Revenue capital duty at the rate of £1 per £100 on the actual value of assets of any kind contributed by the members. Capital duty is chargeable except when shares are allotted partly paid subject to call. A return of allotment of bonus shares should be made on Form No 88(2), on which capital duty is not payable; this should be accompanied by particulars of contract and/ or resolution to capitalise.

---

(10) Increase of capital

A company may increase its capital by passing a resolution authorising the increase (Section 123 of the 1985 Act). A copy of the resolution must be sent to the Registrar within 15 days of its being passed, together with a notice on Form No. 123 giving particulars of the increase. No duty is chargeable on Form No. 123.

---

(11) Share capital consolidation, conversion into stock

If a company having a share capital has converted any shares into stock, etc., it must within one month give notice to the Registrar on Form No 122 (Section 122 of the 1985 Act).

---

(12) Share transfer

A company should not register a transfer of shares in or debentures of the company unless a proper instrument of transfer has been produced (Section 183 of the 1985 Act); this information must be notified in the next annual return. A transfer of shares will normally attract stamp duty and the relevant documents should be sent to:

The Controller Stamps,
Inland Revenue,
Direct Post Section,
West Block,
Barrington Road,
Worthing,
West Sussex BN12 4SF

or to any of the Inland Revenue Stamp Offices listed in

para. 13 below, except the Moorgate Office. Cheques should be drawn in favour of 'Inland Revenue'.

(13) Remittances

Remittances in payment of Inland Revenue capital duties in connection with return of allotments may be sent to the Registrar of Companies, who will arrange for the documents to be stamped by the Inland Revenue. Registrants may, however, themselves get the documents stamped by the Inland Revenue. Facilities are provided in London at the Inland Revenue Stamp Office, Bush House (SW Wing), Strand, London WC2R 1LB, and 61 Moorgate, London EC2R 6BH, and at the Inland Revenue Stamp Offices in Birmingham, Bristol, Cardiff, Edinburgh, Glasgow, Leeds, Liverpool, Manchester, Newcastle-upon-Tyne, Nottingham, and Sheffield. When forms are presented they will be stamped with Inland Revenue duty stamps on payment of the appropriate amount in cash.

Annual General Meetings and Annual Returns

(14) Annual general meetings (companies with share capital) (Companies Act 1985, Sections 363, 365–367)

(i) AGM
An AGM is required to be held within 18 months of incorporation and thereafter every calendar year. 15 months may elapse between AGMs but one must still be held every calendar year.

(ii) AGM year
The annual return must always show the year in which the AGM was actually held – regardless of what year's accounts were presented to the meeting or of what year's business was discussed or of the date(s) of adjourned meeting(s).

NB Accounts can in fact be presented at any general meeting and not necessarily an AGM (Companies Act 1985, Section 241(1) refers). There is no need for more than one AGM or annual return in a calendar year.

(iii) Made-up date
When an AGM is held the made-up date must always be 14 days after the actual date of the meeting.

If no AGM was held in a calendar year, an annual return (with fee) must still be submitted with a made-up date of 31 December of that year.

---

(15) Annual returns

Every company, irrespective of whether or not it is trading, must make an annual return to the Registrar, made up to the fourteenth day after the date of the annual general meeting for the year in question. The return must be filed within 42 days of the meeting. Annual returns forms are available free of charge from the respective Company Registration Offices (see specimen on pp. 120–25). The registration fee on an annual return is £20. All remittances should be made payable to the Registrar of Companies and crossed 'A/c payee'.

NB Failure to forward a copy of the annual return to the Registrar is an offence under Section 365 of the 1985 Act. This is so despite any failure to hold an annual general meeting; in such circumstances, the annual return should be made up to 31 December.

Directors and Secretaries

(16) Directors and secretaries

Details of any change in directors or secretaries of registered companies must be sent to the Registrar on Form No 288 within 14 days of the changes occurring (Sections 288 and 711 of the 1985 Act).

(17) Directors' service contracts

If copies of directors' service contracts, or memorandum thereof, are kept at an address other than the registered office of the company, notification of this address should be sent to the Registrar on Form No 318 (Section 318 of the 1985 Act).

(18) Directors' report

For each financial year the directors shall prepare a report. Reference should be made to Sections 235 and 261, Schedules 7 and 10 of the Companies Act 1985 for full information. Broadly the information required covers development of the business, dividends (if any) they recommend, the amount (if any) that they propose to carry to reserves, the names of the directors, the principal activity of the company, any significant changes in asset values and directors' shareholdings.

(19) Employment of disabled persons

If the average number of employees exceeded 250, the directors' report should include a statement about the policy the company has applied during the financial year to the employment, training, career development

A

COMPANIES FORM No. 363

Annual return of a company

363

Pursuant to sections 363 and 364 of the Companies Act 1985

Note The appropriate fee should accompany this form

Please do not write in this margin

To the Registrar of Companies

For official use

Company number

Please complete legibly, preferably in black type, or bold block lettering

Annual return of (note 1)

*

* insert full name of company

The information in this return is as at

19 †.**(The date of this return** note 1**)**

† if the company has a share capital, this date must be the 14th day after the annual general meeting

Address of registered office of the company

Postcode

Total amount of indebtedness of the company in respect of mortgages and charges (note 2).

£

If different from the registered office, state address where the register of members or any register of debenture holders or any duplicate or part of any register of debentures is kept or may be inspected.

Register of members

Register of debenture holders

Particulars of the secretary

Name (notes 3 and 4)

Previous name(s) (note 3)

Address (notes 4 and 5)

Postcode

‡ only pages 1 and 2 need be completed in the case of a company without share capital

We certify this return which comprises pages 1, 2, [3, 4, 5 and 6]‡ [plus§ ________ continuation sheets]

§ enter number of continuation sheets attached

Signed Director, and Secretary

Presentor's name address and reference (if any):

For official Use

General Section

Post room

Particulars of the director(s) of the company (notes 6 and 7)

Name (note 3)	Business Occupation
Previous name(s) (note 3)	Nationality
Address (note 5)	
	Date of birth (note 9)
Postcode	
Other relevant past or present directorships* (note 8)	

Name (note 3)	Business Occupation
Previous name(s) (note 3)	Nationality
Address (note 5)	
	Date of birth (note 9)
Postcode	
Other relevant past or present directorships* (note 8)	

Name (note 3)	Business Occupation
Previous name(s) (note 3)	Nationality
Address (note 5)	
	Date of birth (note 9)
Postcode	
Other relevant past or present directorships* (note 8)	

Name (note 3)	Business Occupation
Previous name(s) (note 3)	Nationality
Address (note 5)	
	Date of birth (note 9)
Postcode	
Other relevant past or present directorships* (note 8)	

Please do not write in this margin

Please complete legibly, preferably in black type, or bold blocklettering

* delete if inappropriate. Enter particulars of other directorships held or previously held. If this space is insufficient use a continuation sheet

Please do not write in this margin

Summary of share capital and debentures

Nominal share capital	£		
	Number of shares	Class	Nominal value of each share
divided into:- 1			£
2			£
3			£

Please complete legibly, preferably in black type, or bold block lettering

Issued share capital and debentures

		Amount per share	Number	Class
1.Number of shares of each class taken up to the date of this return.	1			
	2			
	3			
2.Number of shares of each class issued subject to payment wholly in cash	1			
	2			
	3			
3.Number of shares of each class issued as fully paid up for aconsideration other than cash	1			
	2			
	3			
4.Number of shares of each class issued as partly paid up for a consideration other than cash and extent to which each such share is so paid up	1	£		
	2	£		
	3	£		
5.Number of shares (if any) of each class issued at a discount	1			
	2			
	3			

Continued on page 4

LIST OF PAST

Folio in register ledger containing particulars	Names and Addresses	
		1
		2
		3
		4
		5
		6
		7
		8
		9
		10
		11
		12
		13
		14
		15

Please do not write in this margin

Please complete legibly, preferably black type, or bold block lettering

Summary of share capital and debentures continued

	Amount	Number	Class	
6 Amount of discount on the issue of shares which has not been written off at the date of this return	£			
7 Amount per share called up on number of shares of each class	£			1
	£			2
	£			3
8 Total amount of calls received (note 10)	£			
9 Total amount (if any) agreed to be considered as paid on number of shares of each class issued as fully paid up for a consideration other than cash	£			1
	£			2
	£			3
10 Total amount (if any) agreed to be considered as paid on number of shares of each class issued as partly paid up for a consideration other than cash	£			1
	£			2
	£			3
11 Total amount of calls unpaid	£			
12 Total amount of sums (if any) paid by way of commission in respect of any shares or debentures	£			
13 Total amount of the sums (if any) allowed by way of discount for any debentures since the date of the last return	£			
14 Total number of shares of each class forfeited				1
				2
				3
15 Total amount paid (if any) on shares forfeited	£			
16 Total amount of shares for which share warrants to bearer are outstanding	£			
17 Total amount of share warrants to bearer issued and surrendered respectively since the date of the last return — ISSUED	£			
SURRENDERED	£			
18 Number of shares comprised in each share warrant to bearer, specifying in the case of warrants of different kinds, particulars of each kind				

AND PRESENT MEMBERS (notes 11 and 12)

Account of Shares					
Number of shares or amount of stock held by existing members at date of return (note 11)	Particulars of shares transferred since the date of the last return,or,in the case of the first return,of the incorporation of the company,by (a) persons who are still members,and (b) persons who have ceased to be members (note 12)			Remarks	
	Number	Date of Registration of transfer (a)	(b)		
					1
					2
					3
					4
					5
					6
					7
					8
					9
					10
					11
					12
					13
					14
					15

LIST OF PAST

Folio in register ledger containing Particulars	Names and addresses	
		16
		17
		18
		19
		20
		21
		22
		23
		24
		25
		26
		27
		28
		29
		30

Notes

1. An annual return is required for every calendar year. If the company has a share capital the date of this return must be the 14th day after the date of the annual general meeting. If it does not have a share capital the date of this return must be a date not more than 42 days after the annual general meeting

2. This section should include only indebtedness in respect of charges (whenever created) of any description set out in section 396(1) of the Companies Act 1985 (in the case of English and Welsh companies) or section 410(4) of that Act (in the case of Scottish companies).

3. For an individual, his present christian name(s) and surname must be given, together with any previous christian name(s) or surname(s).

   "Christian name" includes a forename. In the case of a peer or person usually known by a title different from his surname, "surname" means that title. In the case of a corporation, its corporate name must be given.

   A previous christian name or surname need not be given if:—

   (a) in the case of a married woman, it was a name by which she was known before her marriage; or

   (b) it was changed or ceased to be used at least 20 years ago, or before the person who previously used it reached the age of 18; or

   (c) in the case of a peer or a person usually known by a British title different from his surname, it was a name by which he was known before he adopted the title or succeeded to it

4. Where all the partners in a firm are joint secretaries, only the firm name and its principal office need be given.

   Where the secretary or one of the joint secretaries is a Scottish firm, give only the firm name and its principal office.

5. Usual residential address must be given. In the case of a corporation, give the registered or principal office.

6. Director includes any person who occupies the position of a director, by whatever name called, and any person in accordance with whose directions or instructions the directors of the company are accustomed to act.

7. If the space provided for listing directors is inadequate, a prescribed continuation sheet must be used.

8. The names must be given of all bodies corporate incorporated in Great Britain of which the director is also a director, or has been a director at any time during the preceeding five years.

   However a present or past directorship need not be disclosed if it is, or has been, held in a body corporate which, throughout that directorship, has been:—

   (a) a dormant company (which is a company which has had no transactions required to be entered in the company's accounting records, except any which may have arisen from the taking of shares in the company by a subscriber to the memorandum as such).

   (b) a body corporate of which the company making the return was a wholly-owned subsidiary;

AND PRESENT MEMBERS Continued (notes 11 and 12)

Account of Shares					
Number of shares or amount of stock held by existing members at date of return (note 11)	Particulars of shares transferred since the date of the last return, or, in the case of the first return, of the incorporation of the company, by (a) persons who are still members, and (b) persons who have ceased to be members (note 12)			Remarks	
	Number	Date of Registration of transfer (a)	(b)		
					16
					17
					18
					19
					20
					21
					22
					23
					24
					25
					26
					27
					28
					29
					30

(c) a wholly-owned subsidiary of the company making the return; or

(d) a wholly-owned subsidiary of a body corporate of which the company making the return was also a wholly owned subsidiary.

9. Dates of birth need only be given if the company making the return is:—

   (a) a public company;
   (b) the subsidiary of a public company; or
   (c) the subsidiary of a public company registered in Northern Ireland

10. Include payments on application and allotment, and any sums received or shares forfeited.

11. Show all the persons currently holding shares or stock in the company at the date of the return, giving their names and addresses, the number of shares or amount of stock held, and details of all transfers since the last return or, if this is the first annual return of the company, all transfers since the company was incorporated. If more than one class of share is held please add more columns as appropriate.

    Additionally, show all persons and their relevant details if they have ceased to be members since the last return was made, or if this is the first return, since the company was incorporated.

    If the list of members is not in alphabetical order, an index which will enable any member to be readily located within the list must be attached to this return. If the space provided for listing members is inadequate, a prescribed continuation sheet is available.

    If full details have been given on the return for either of the last two years, a company may, if it so wishes, only include in this section details relating to persons who since the date of the last return:
    (a) have become members;
    (b) have ceased to be members; or
    (c) are existing members whose holdings of stock or shares have changed.
    If full details have been given on the return for either of the last two years and there have been no changes please state "No Change".

12. For consistency, it is suggested that particulars should be placed opposite the name of the transferor and not opposite that of the transferee, but the name of the transferee may be inserted in the remarks column opposite the particulars of each transfer.

ZP 54-1809 6 85

and promotion of disabled persons (Statutory Instrument No 1160 of 1980 – The Companies (Directors' Report) (Employment of Disabled Persons) Regulations 1980).

(20) Register of directors' interests

Every company must keep a register for the purposes of Sections 324–328 of the 1985 Act, which requires directors to notify the company within five days of any interests they, their spouses or their infant children have in shares or debentures of the company, its holding company or any subsidiary (Section 328 of the 1985 Act). If this register is not kept at the registered office of the company, then a notification of the address at which it is kept, and any changes in that address, must be sent to the Registrar on Form No 325 or No 325A if the register is kept in non-legible form (on computer tape or disc). Schedule 13 Part I of the 1985 Act contains provisions for giving effect to Sections 324, 732, Schedule 13 Parts II, III, and explains what 'interest' means. A company listed on a recognised stock exchange must notify that stock exchange of any acquisition or disposal by a director of such of its shares or debentures as are listed on that stock exchange. Notification must be made by the following day, excluding a Saturday, Sunday or bank holiday (Section 329 of the 1985 Act).

(21) Disqualification of directors

The Secretary of State has the power to apply to the court for an order disqualifying a person from acting as a director of a company for up to five years if he has been persistently in default in relation to the relevant requirements of the Acts. Being adjudged guilty of three or more defaults in filing returns, accounts or other documents to the Registrar within a period of five years would be proof of persistent default (Section

299 of the 1985 Act). A public register of disqualified persons, including those disqualified under Sections 295–300 Schedule 12 of the 1985 Act is open to inspection on payment of a fee at the following addresses (Section 301 of the 1985 Act):

Companies Registration Office
Companies House
Crown Way
Maindy
Cardiff CF4 3UZ

The Insolvency Service
Thomas Moore Buildings
Royal Courts of Justice
Strand
London WC2A 2JY

London Search Room
Companies House
55–71 City Road
London EC1Y 1BB

Companies Registration Office
Exchequer Chambers
102 George Street
Edinburgh EH2 3DJ

(22) Secretary's qualifications

See sections 283 and 286 of the Companies Act 1985.

Auditors

(23) Qualifications

An auditor must either be a member of one of the following recognised accountancy bodies:

- the Institute of Chartered Accountants in England and Wales
- the Institute of Chartered Accountants of Scotland
- the Association of Certified Accountants
- the Institute of Chartered Accountants in Ireland

or have been authorised by the Secretary of State under Section 398 of the 1985 Act.

(24) Appointment and removal

Every company is required to appoint auditors at each general meeting at which accounts are laid and these auditors shall hold office until the end of the next such meeting. Automatic reappointment of auditors is no longer permitted. Where the company or its directors fail to appoint or reappoint auditors, the Secretary of State may appoint a person to fill the vacancy. An auditor may be removed on or before the expiration of the term of office, subject to certain provisions (Sections 384–388 of the 1985 Act).

(25) Resignation

An auditor who resigns is required to deposit at the registered office of the company a statement in writing whether or not there are circumstances connected with his resignation that should be brought to the attention of shareholders or creditors. If there are such circumstances, the auditor is required to say what they are, and a copy of his statement must be sent by the company to every person entitled to receive a copy of the company's accounts, and be filed with the Registrar within 14 days. Where a retiring auditor makes a statement, the auditor may call on the directors to convene an extraordinary meeting to receive and consider such explanation of the circumstances in connection with his resignation as he may wish to make. A 'nil' return is also required to be filed (Sections 390 and 391 of the 1985 Act).

(26) Powers in relation to subsidiaries

Where a holding company has a subsidiary that is

incorporated in Great Britain, it is the duty of that subsidiary and its auditors to give to the auditors of the holding company such information as those auditors may reasonably require (Section 392 of the 1985 Act).

(27) False statements, etc., to auditors

It is a criminal offence for an officer of a company knowingly and recklessly to make false or misleading statements to an auditor (Section 393 of the 1985 Act).

Resolutions

(28) Resolutions

Where a company is required to file with the Registrar a copy of a resolution it has passed (these are, in the main, special or extraordinary resolutions increasing capital), filing must take place within 15 days of the passing of the resolution (Sections 123, 380 and 572 of the 1985 Act) and should be accompanied by the altered Memorandum and Articles of Association as in paras 29 and 30 below.

(29) Alterations of Memorandum of Association

A company may alter its objects within the limits laid down in Sections 4, 5 and 6 of the 1985 Act. It must pass a special resolution to do so, a copy of which has to be sent to the Registrar within 15 days of it being passed (Sections 380–572 of the 1985 Act).

If there is no application to the court for the alteration to be cancelled, the company must, within 15 days from the end of the period for making such an application, send to the Registrar a printed copy of its Memorandum as altered. An application to the court for the alteration to be cancelled must be made within 21 days of the date of passing the resolution, and notice of the application given to the Registrar forthwith on Form No 6. An office copy of the court order cancelling or confirming the alteration must be sent to the Registrar within 15 days of the order. If the order confirms the alteration, the office copy thereof, when sent to the Registrar, must be accompanied by a printed copy of the Memorandum as altered (Sections 4, 5 and 6 of the 1985 Act).

When an alteration is made in the company's memorandum other than under Sections 4, 5 and 6 of the 1985 Act, a copy of the document making or evidencing the alteration must be sent to the Registrar within 15 days of it having been passed together with a printed copy of the Memorandum as altered.

---

(30) Alteration of Articles of Association

A company may alter its Articles of Association by passing a special resolution specifying which clauses have been altered. A copy of the special resolution must be sent to the Registrar as in para. 29 above.

---

(31) Adoption of new Memorandum or Articles

Resolutions to adopt new Memorandum or Articles must have the new Memorandum or Articles attached to the resolution. In cases where the new Memorandum is adopted, a printed copy must be sent to the Registrar as in para. 29 above.

---

(32) Printing requirements

See Chapter 3, section 3.15.

(33) Prospectus

Sections 56–58, 61–62 and 64–71 of the 1985 Act deal with the issue of a prospectus. Two copies of every prospectus, duly dated and signed, must be filed with the Registrar on or before the date of its publication.

A document containing an offer of shares or debentures for sale to the public shall be deemed to be a prospectus.

(34) Change of name

A company may by special resolution and with the approval of the Secretary of State change its name. The resolution should be accompanied by a remittance of £40 in payment of the registration fee (Section 28 of the 1985 Act).

(35) Mortgage debentures and other charges

(i) Particulars of certain mortgages or charges created by a company must be delivered on Form 395 (or, in the case of debentures or debenture stock, on Form 397) to the Registrar within 21 days of the date of their creation together with the relevant instrument (if any) creating the charge (Sections 395–398 of the 1985 Act). Where more than one issue is made of debentures in a series, particulars of each further issue must be sent to the Registrar on Form 397(a).

(ii) A charge is considered to be registrable under Sections 395–398 of the Act if the description of the property charges falls within Section 396 of the Act.

(iii) Particulars of certain mortgages or charges

existing on property acquired by a company must also be delivered to the Registrar on Form 400 within 21 days of the acquisition, together with a certified copy of the instrument (if any) that created the charge (Section 400).

(iv) The registration of mortgages and charges by companies registered at the Edinburgh Office and on property, etc., situated in Scotland may involve other requirements about which the Registrar for Scotland should be consulted.

(v) Particulars of a charge created by an English company over property in Scotland or Northern Ireland are required to be presented to the Registrar in England within 21 days of it having been recorded at the Registry of Sasines in Edinburgh or the Deeds Registry in Belfast, as the case may be.

(vi) A certificate is issued in respect of every charge registered under the 1985 Act (Section 401) and a copy of this certificate is to be endorsed on debentures or certificates of debenture stock (Section 402).

(vii) Failure to deliver particulars (and relevant instruments) to the Registrar within the 21-day time limit mentioned above will result in the charge becoming void against the liquidator and any creditor of the company in respect of charges created by the company (Sections 395–398) and in penalties on the company and its officers whether the charge is already in existence under Section 400 or is created by the company under Sections 395–398. The court may in appropriate circumstances and subject to such conditions as thought fit extend the time (Section 404).

(viii) When a charge is wholly or partly satisfied or the property charge is released or no longer forms part of the undertaking of the company, a memorandum of satisfaction may be filed under Section 403 on either Form 403a or 403b. It should be noted when completing the forms that the two officers of the company present at the declaration must sign the form against the declaration and two officers of the company must sign against the seal of the company. It should also be noted that the date of the swearing of the declaration must not precede the date of sealing. A copy of every instrument creating a charge requiring registration under the Act is to be kept at the company's registered office (Section 406).

(ix) The register of charges kept by a company and the copies of instruments creating mortgages and charges are available for public inspection (Sections 407 and 408).

---

(36) Register of debenture holders

If a company keeps its register of debenture holders at an address other than its registered office, notification of the address at which it is kept, and any changes in that address, must be sent to the Registrar on Form No 190 or on Form No 190a if the register is kept in non-legible form (on computer tape/disc) (Section 190 of the 1985 Act).

Defaults and Winding-up

(37) Defaults

The Companies Acts provide for the imposition of penalties for various defaults in carrying out the requirements of the Acts. Directors and officers of a company are personally responsible if such defaults occur, whether or not the preparation of returns, etc., has been deputed to accountants or other parties.

(38) Defunct companies

The Registrar has the power to strike companies off the register when he has reason to believe that they are not carrying out business or in operation (Sections 652–653 of the 1985 Act).

The Registrar will also consider striking a company off the register if he is asked to do so when the company is no longer required (see also para. 39 below).

(39) Winding-up

The winding up of a company under the 1985 Act may be by:

- the court (Section 517);
- members voluntarily (Sections 579–586);
- creditors voluntarily (Sections 587–595);
- subject to the supervision of the court (Section 606).

Notice of a meeting of creditors called for the purpose of Section 588 must be advertised once in the *London Gazette* (in the case of companies registered in England and Wales) and once at least in two local newspapers circulating in the district of the registered office or principal place of business of the company. Notice of all resolutions to wind up voluntarily must be given within 14 days after their passing, by advertisement in the *London Gazette* (in the case of companies registered in England and Wales) (Section 573). A copy of the resolution to wind up voluntarily must be filed with the Registrar within 15 days of the passing of the resolution (Sections 380 and 572).

In the case of a proposal to wind up a company as a members' voluntary winding up, a meeting of the directors should first be called at which a 'declaration of solvency' must be made. This declaration should include a statement of the company's assets and liabilities as at the latest practicable date before the declaration is made. This document is a preliminary to the members of the company formally resolving to wind up (Sections 577–578).

The declaration of solvency must:

- be made within five weeks before the date of passing the resolution to wind up, and
- be filed with the Registrar at least before the resolution is passed.

Failure to comply with these two requirements will, in the view of the provisions of Sections 577–578, result in an intended members' voluntary winding up having to be treated as a creditors' voluntary winding up.

Notes for guidance on voluntary liquidation may be obtained free from the Registrar on request.

Letters, Trade Catalogues, etc.

(40) Obligation to exhibit certain information

(i) A company shall not state, in any form, the name of any of its directors (otherwise than in the text or as a signatory) on any business letter on which the company's name appears unless it states on the letter in legible characters the Christian name, or the initials thereof, and the surname of every director of the company who is an individual and the corporate name of every corporate director. It is, therefore, a requirement that a company shall not publish the name of any of its directors unless it publishes the names of them all.

(ii) Every company must show its name in legible characters on all business letters of the company and on all notices and other official publications of the company, and on bills of exchange, promissory notes, endorsements, cheques and orders for money or goods purporting to be signed on behalf of the company, and on all bills of parcels, invoices, receipts and letters of credit of the company (Sections 348–350 of the 1985 Act).

(iii) In addition, companies are required to show under Section 351 of the Companies Act 1985 on business letters and order forms:

(a) The place of registration of the company, and the number with which it is registered. It is recommended that the place of registration should be indicated by printing any one of the following on its stationery:

- Registered in England and Wales
- Registered in Cardiff
- Registered in Wales

Companies using the expression 'England' or 'London' for these purposes need not change their letter paper as a result of the move of the Companies Registration Office to Cardiff. For companies registered in Scotland, 'registered in Scotland' or 'registered in Edinburgh' would be acceptable. The registered number of a company is shown on its certificate of incorporation.

(b) The address of its registered office. If a business letter or an order form shows more than one address, it is advisable, to avoid confusion, to indicate which of them is the address of the registered office. Where it shows only the address of the registered office, the fact that that is the address of the registered office must be stated.

(c) In the case of a limited company that is exempt under Sections 30–31 of the 1985 Act from the obligation to use the word 'Limited' as part of its name, the fact that it is a limited company. This does not alter the company's right to omit the word 'Limited' from its name.

(iv) If there is any reference to the amount of share capital on any business letter or order form, the reference must be paid-up share capital. A reference to share capital is not, however, obligatory.

(41) Registered office

Details of any changes in the situation of a company's registered office must be sent to the Registrar on Form No 287 within 14 days of the changes occurring (Sections 10, 287 and 711 of the 1985 Act).

(42) Register of members

Every company must keep a register of members containing the names and addresses of members and particulars of shares held by each (Sections 191(7) and 352–353 of the 1985 Act). The date on which each person was entered in the register, and when he ceased to be a member, must also be shown.

The register is normally kept at the registered office of the company, but, if not, the Registrar must be notified on Form No 353 of the address at which it is kept (and of any changes in that address), or on Form 353a if the register is kept in non-legible form (on computer tape/disc).

(43) Register of substantial interest in a company

Section 33 of the 1967 Act as amended by Section 328, Schedule 13 Part II of the 1985 Act requires all persons having an interest in shares of a company with a stock exchange listing to notify the company accordingly within five days. Every company to which the section applies must keep a register for the purposes of recording these particulars. The register must be kept at the same address as the place where the register of directors' interests is kept (see para. 20). The provisions of Schedule 13 Part I of the 1985 Act are applied with certain variations. Listed companies have the right to require registered shareholders to disclose whether or not they are the beneficial owners of shares, and, if not, who else has an interest in the shares (Sections 324, 732, Schedule 13 Parts II, III).

(44) Company seal

Every company shall have its name engraved in legible characters on its seal (Section 350 of the 1985 Act).

(45) Protection afforded to persons dealing with a company

A company may not reply against other persons on:

(i) the making of a winding-up order,
(ii) any alteration in its Memorandum or Articles,
(iii) any change in its directors or in the address of its registered office in relation to the service of documents of the company,
(iv) the appointment of a liquidator in a voluntary winding-up,

if the event has not been officially notified at the material time, unless the company can prove that it was known at the material time to the other party. If the event is officially notified less than 15 days before the material time, the other party may treat it as ineffective against him by showing that he was unavoidably prevented knowing of it.

'Officially notified' means, as regards (i), (ii) and (iii) above, notice to the *London Gazette* by the Registrar of the receipt of documents evidencing the event and, as regards (iv), notice in the *London Gazette* by the liquidator of his appointment.

(46) Inspection of company documents

All documents kept by the Registrar relative to individual companies may be inspected at either Companies House, Crown Way, Maindy, Cardiff CF4 3UZ, or the

London Search Room, Companies House, 55–71 City Road, London EC1Y 1BB (see Appendix B for further details).

(47) Companies with registered offices in Wales
Any company whose Memorandum states that its registered office is situated in Wales may submit documents to the Registrar in Welsh, provided that they are accompanied by a certified English translation. Such companies may also alter 'Limited' to 'Cyfyngedig' as the last word in their name without seeking the approval of the Secretary of State for Trade. However, a certificate of incorporation on change of name must be obtained from the Registrar; no fee will be charged (Sections 2, 21, 25, 351 of the 1985 Act).

(48) Unlimited companies
An unlimited company is exempted by Sections 227, 239, 241, 711, 742 and 744 of the 1985 Act from the requirement to file its accounts and the directors' report with its annual return, provided that the company is not:

- a subsidiary of one (or more) limited companies
- a holding company of a limited company
- carrying on business as a promoter of a trading stamp scheme.

(49) Overseas companies
Companies incorporated outside Great Britain that have established a place of business in Great Britain

are obliged to register certain documents with the Registrar (Section 691 of the 1985 Act). Detailed information about these requirements and the need to register mortgages, debentures and other charges can be obtained on request from the Registrar.

(50) Dominion register

A company having a share capital whose objects comprise the transaction of business in any part of Her Majesty's dominions outside Great Britain, the Channel Islands or the Isle of Man may keep in any such part of Her Majesty's dominions in which it transacts business a branch register of members resident in that part.

The company shall give notice to the Registrar in Form No 362, or Form No 362a if the register is kept in non-legible form (on computer disc/tape), of the situation of the office where any dominion register is kept and of any change in its situation, and of its discontinuance within 14 days of the event (Section 362, Schedule 14 Parts I, II, para. 1 of the 1985 Act).

(51) Mergers and amalgamations

Under Sections 428–430 of the Companies Act 1985, when a company (the 'transferee company') has made an offer for the shares of another (the 'transferor company') and obtained 90 per cent of the total share capital of the transferor company, it must notify the remaining shareholders of that fact on Form No 429(2). Those shareholders may give notice to the transferee company (on Form No 429(3)) requiring that it acquire their holdings in the transferor company.

If within four months of the offer being made the transferee company obtains 90 per cent of the shares for which the offer was made (i.e. excluding the transferee's holdings before the offer was made), it may give notice to the remaining shareholders (on Form

No 428) of that fact, and gain legal rights to acquire the holdings of those shareholders.

If notices are given on Forms No 428 or 429(3), the transferee company must acquire the shares on the basis of the offer as previously made. If notice is given on Form No 428, the shareholder has a right to apply to the court to establish a proper consideration for the transfer of his shares. If notice is given on Form No 429(3), either the shareholder or the transferee company may apply to the court to establish a proper consideration for the transfer.

Any notice to be given to the transferee company shall be as follows:

(i) Any notice to be given pursuant to Sections 428–430 to a shareholder in a transferor company shall be given to him personally or by sending it by post to him, but where this cannot be done because the shareholder is the holder of a share warrant to bearer the notice shall be given:

- in cases where the Articles of Association or regulations of the transferor company provide that notice to such shareholders may be given by advertisement, by advertisement in the manner so provided;

- in any other case, by means of an advertisement in the *Gazette*.

(ii) where in accordance with (i) above a notice has to be sent by post it shall be sent to the shareholder:

- at his address in the United Kingdom registered in the books of the transferor company, or,

- if no address in the United Kingdom is so registered, at the address if any within the United Kingdom supplied by him to the transferor company for the giving of notices to him, or,

- if no address in the United Kingdom is registered or has been so notified, at his address outside the United Kingdom registered in the books of the transferor company.

If a notice is sent to an address in the United Kingdom it shall be sent by recorded delivery post but otherwise it shall be sent by airmail post.

(52) Fees payable to Registrar

The Secretary of State has power to prescribe fees paid to be paid to the Registrar of Companies (Section 708 of the 1985 Act).

(53) Company name outside business premises

Every company shall paint or affix and keep painted or affixed its name on the outside of every office or place in which its business is carried on, in a conspicuous position in letters easily legible (Section 348 of the 1985 Act).

Appendix B

The Work of the Companies Registration Office

Examination and Filing of Documents

The documents that require to be filed for examination fall into four main categories:

(i) All companies must submit annual returns and accounts to the Registrar. (Certain unlimited companies are exempt from the requirement to file annual accounts – see Appendix A, para. 5(i)(b).) Failure to comply with these obligations is an offence and defaulting companies and/or their officers are liable to be referred for prosecution or, if companies appear to be no longer in business or operation, removal from the register.

(ii) Companies are required to notify the Registrar of changes in their circumstances, e.g. change of registered office address, directors, capital structure, etc.

(iii) Particulars of mortgages and charges created by companies must be delivered to the Registrar within strict time limits if the lenders wish to retain their security as creditors in a liquidation. Memoranda of satisfaction may also be filed, but this is not a statutory requirement.

(iv) Special conditions apply when a company is wound up. Notices of the appointment and release of receivers and liquidators, together with their statutory returns and accounts, and the arrangements for dissolution when a liquidation is completed, must be notified to the Registrar.

Associated with the work of examining is action on alleged specific breaches of the Companies Acts. The Registrar exercises on behalf of the Secretary of State certain discretions, under the Acts, to companies. The Registrar has responsibility for the administration of other Acts, including the Newspaper Libel and Registration Act 1881 and the Limited Partnerships Act 1907. In addition, he holds records of companies formed under Special Railway, Canal and Assurance Acts, Charters, etc. and companies that are incorporated overseas but have a place of business in England or Wales. Following the repeal of the Registration of Business Names Act 1916 on 26 February 1982, the Registrar, on behalf of the Secretary of State, has assumed responsibility for the approval of the use of certain proscribed words or expressions in business names. Court action may also be taken against business owners who fail to comply with the ownership disclosure requirements of the Business Names Act 1985.

Public Search

Information filed by companies registered in England and Wales is available on microfiche at the Public Search Rooms of Companies House, Crown Way, Maindy, Cardiff CF4 3UZ and Companies House,

55–71 City Road, London ED1Y 1BB. The original paper documents, with the exception of mortgage and incorporation documents, are no longer filed on the traditional 'hard-backed' company files, but are available on special request. Photocopies of documents can also be obtained. There are fees for these services. The offices are open to the public on Mondays to Fridays (excluding public holidays) from 9.30 a.m. to 4.00 p.m. in Cardiff, and from 9.45 a.m. to 4.00 p.m. in London. Requests for searches are normally accepted up to 15 minutes before closing time.

From 1 December 1983, uncertified copies of company records have been available by post from the Companies Registration Office at Cardiff. These records can be provided either as microfiche or as photostat copies. Requests for further information on this service and its current costs should be made to Postal Search Section, Companies House, Crown Way, Maindy, Cardiff CF4 3UZ.

The Alphabetical Index of Companies and the CRO Directory of Companies (including regular updates) may be viewed, free of charge, at the Public Search Rooms in Cardiff and London. The Index lists the names and registration numbers of companies registered in England and Wales, Scotland and Northern Ireland. The Directory gives additional information such as the registered office address, date of incorporation, 'made-up' dates of the latest annual returns and accounts filed.

Both the Index and Directory (including updates) can be purchased in magnetic tape (for users with computer facilities), roll film or microfiche form. Paper copies of the Index or Directory are not provided.

A guide to the Index of companies

As from January 1976, the index of names and registration numbers of all live companies together with changes of name and dissolutions occurring after

January 1976 are presented on microfilm; only details of companies that were dissolved or changed their name prior to January 1976 will continue to be shown on the special strip or card index.

Form of the microfilm index

The alphabetical sequence of the index has been divided for convenience into four groups, namely A–D, E–K, L–R, and S–Z, each of which is presented on separate cassette viewers. The index is updated and cassettes replaced at the beginning of each month, and within each month two cumulative daily supplements are prepared, the first giving details of company names added to the index, the second giving names of companies removed from the index by change of name or dissolution.

Content of the microfilm index

The microfilm index lists all live companies registered in England and Wales, Scotland and Northern Ireland. The company records of the last two categories, denoted in the index by the code letters 'SC' or 'NI', are held in Edinburgh and Belfast. Companies dissolved during the current calendar year are indicated by the code letter 'D', whilst changes of names are coded 'C' (in such cases, both new and old names are shown during the current calendar year). Other code letters, as shown on the notices displayed in the Index Room, denote other categories of company records.

Alphabetical listing

All company names are listed in strict alphabetical order (full account being taken of any initials) with the exception of those names commencing 'The'. In such cases, whether or not the remainder of the name is in inverted commas, the indexing takes place on the letter immediately following 'The'. For example, 'The Guardian' or 'The "Guardian"' will be found under G, whilst 'F. W. Woolworth Ltd' will be found under F.

FIGURES, ETC.

(i) Figures are translated into words digit by digit. Thus '1908' is presented as 'one-nine-o-eight', '11' is 'one-one' and '17' is 'one-seven'.
(ii) Roman numerals are treated as ordinary letters of the alphabet.
(iii) Symbols and signs are ignored with the exception of the ampersand (&) and the percentage sign (%) which are treated as if they were written 'and' or 'per cent' respectively.
(iv) Mac, Mc, M', St and Saint are indexed in strict alphabetical sequence.

Additional service

Copies of the live index, in either of two forms, are available for purchase and personal collection by yearly subscription as follows:

(i) Main index in reels of film for use in cassette readers and the daily supplement on microfiche.
(ii) Main index and daily supplement all in microfiche form.

In both cases, the annual charge is payable in advance with order. This charge is subject to review and does not include any possible liability to VAT or any postage charges.

Operation of the cassette readers

MOVEMENT OF THE FILM

The images (pages) are recorded sequentially on a roll of film held in a cassette. To move the film forwards or backwards, press the appropriately marked red button located on the front of the reader. The film drive operates at two speeds, depending on the pressure on the button. Movement of a few pages is best effected by using the hand wheel mounted on the left-hand side of the reader: use the small one first, and then the larger one for a final adjustment.

FILM INDEXING

The film is indexed by means of a dark band which, when the film is moving, travels up or down the screen. The position of the band against the scale fixed to the side of the screen indicates which section of the alphabet is being displayed.

FOCUS

To focus the image, turn the thumb wheel located to the left of the drive buttons.

Operation of the microfiche readers

MOVEMENT OF THE MICROFILM

The microfiche consists of a grid pattern of images, arranged in sequence. The microfiche can be moved in any direction by using the black knob on the fiche carrier, which is located below the screen.

MICROFICHE INDEXING

Any page in the grid can be displayed by moving the pointer to the corresponding marking on the index plate.

FOCUS

To adjust the focus, rotate the knob located on the side of the reader to the bottom right-hand side of the screen.

Further information on this service can be obtained from Computer Liaison Section, Companies House, Crown Way, Maindy, Cardiff CF4 3UZ.

Fees Charged by Companies Registration Office

Incorporations	£50	as from December 1973
Change of company names	£40	as from December 1973
Annual returns	£20	due from any return received on or after 2 June 1975
Search fee	£1	as from 1 April 1981
Photocopies	10p per sheet	

Annual Workload of the CRO

	Number of companies on the register at the end of year	*Searches of company records by the public or their agents*	*Official searches of company records*	*Accounts filed*	*Annual returns filed*	*New incorporations during the year*	*Change of name certificates issued*	*Mortgage documents registered*	*Removals from the register*	
									Under S353 or C/A 1948	*Others*
1977	673,020	2,113,000	438,780		438,238	52,872	15,502	73,517	31,598	7,423
1978	727,839	2,327,000	417,470	399,947	419,049	60,611	15,754	83,231	16,839	7,345
1979	757,926	2,108,800	324,497	441,568	467,423	62,958	17,821	79,403	17,330	6,582
1980	789,865	2,665,389	361,307	439,834	468,683	66,104	22,588	81,722	20,558	5,351
1981	830,727	1,136,807	117,743	401,396	424,423	68,941	24,573	78,726	22,217	6,068
1982	862,001	1,898,425	278,210	438,728	465,104	82,955	32,312	96,601	46,200	5,815
1983	910,765	2,160,944	295,015	529,306	570,547	91,470	35,632	103,249	34,114	8,909

Dear Reader,
Many corporations are started by solicitors and 'formation specialists'. Not only are their fees high, but they only give you your Certificate of Incorporation, Mem & Arts, company seal and a register. They do not give you the inner workings for your corporation.

The purpose of this book has been to acquaint you with the formalities of forming your own corporation at the lowest possible cost. It has also led you into the workings of a corporation and given you an insight into offshore formalities.

If you are just starting off in business I suggest you read as many business books as possible. Your public library carries many good ones. If you find a particular book needs to be permanently on your bookshelf, then go out and buy it.

I feel sure that once you have formed your own corporation you will refer back to this book on many occasions.

If I have saved you money or given you any help or a greater insight into corporations generally – then I have succeeded.

My sincere wishes go with you.

BMS

Index